YOUTH AND LIFE

YOUTH AND LIFE

BY

RANDOLPH S. BOURNE

Essay Index Reprint Series

BOOKS FOR LIBRARIES PRESS
FREEPORT, NEW YORK

First Published 1913
Reprinted 1967

INTERNATIONAL STANDARD BOOK NUMBER:
0-8369-0229-7

LIBRARY OF CONGRESS CATALOG CARD NUMBER:
67-23184

PRINTED IN THE UNITED STATES OF AMERICA
BY
NEW WORLD BOOK MANUFACTURING CO., INC.
HALLANDALE, FLORIDA 33009

CONTENTS

I

YOUTH

YOUTH AND LIFE

I

YOUTH

How shall I describe Youth, the time of contradictions and anomalies? The fiercest radicalisms, the most dogged conservatisms, irrepressible gayety, bitter melancholy, — all these moods are equally part of that showery springtime of life. One thing, at least, it clearly is: a great, rich rush and flood of energy. It is as if the store of life had been accumulating through the slow, placid years of childhood, and suddenly the dam had broken and the waters rushed out, furious and uncontrolled, before settling down into the quieter channels of middle life. The youth is suddenly seized with a poignant consciousness of being alive, which is quite wanting to the naïve unquestioning existence of the child. He finds himself overpoweringly urged toward self-expression. Just as the baby, born into a "great, blooming, buzzing confusion," and attracted by every movement, every color, every sound, kicks madly in response in all

3

directions, and only gradually gets his movements coördinated into the orderly and precise movements of his elders, — so the youth suddenly born into a confusion of ideas and appeals and traditions responds in the most chaotic way to this new spiritual world, and only gradually learns to find his way about in it, and get his thoughts and feelings into some kind of order.

Fortunate the young man who does not make his entrance into too wide a world. And upon the width and depth of that new world will depend very much whether his temperament is to be radical or conservative, adventurous or conventional. For it is one of the surprising things about youth that it can so easily be the most conservative of all ages. Why do we suppose that youth is always radical? At no age are social proprieties more strictly observed, and Church, State, law, and order, more rigorously defended. But I like to think that youth is conservative only when its spiritual force has been spent too early, or when the new world it enters into is found, for some reason, to be rather narrow and shallow. It is so often the urgent world of pleasure that first catches the eye of youth; its flood of life is drawn off in that direction; the boy may fritter away his precious birthright in pure lightness of heart and animal spirits. And it is only too true that this type of youth is transitory. Pleasure contrives to burn itself out very quickly, and youth finds itself left prematurely with the ashes of middle age. But if, in some way, the flood of life is checked in the direction of pleasure, then it bursts forth in another, — in the direction of ideals; then we say that the boy is radical. Youth is always turbulent, but the momentous difference is whether it shall be turbulent in passion or in enthusiasm. Nothing is so pathetic as the young man who spends his spiritual force too early, so that when the world of ideals is presented to him, his force being spent, he can only grasp at secondhand ideals and mouldy formulas.

This is the great divergence which sets youth not only against old age, but against youth itself: the undying spirit of youth that seems to be fed by an unquenchable fire, that does not burn itself out but seems to grow steadier and steadier as life goes on, against the fragile, quickly tarnished type that passes relentlessly into middle life. At twenty-five I find myself full of the wildest radicalisms, and look with dismay at my childhood friends who are already settled down, have achieved babies and responsibilities, and have somehow got ten years beyond me in a day. And this divergence shows itself in a thousand different ways. It may be a temptation to a world of pleasure, it may be a sheltering from the stimulus of ideas, or even a sluggish temperament, that separates traditional and adventurous youth, but fundamentally it is a question of how youth takes the world. And here I find that I can no longer drag the traditional youth along with me in this paper. There are many of him, I know, but I do not like him, and I know nothing about him. Let us rather look at the way radical youth grows into and meets the world.

From the state of "the little child, to whom the sky is a roof of blue, the world a screen of opaque and disconnected facts, the home a thing eternal, and 'being good' just simple obedience to unquestioned authority," one steps suddenly into that "vast world of adult perception, pierced deep by flaring search-lights of partial understanding."

The child has an utter sense of security; childhood is unconscious even that it is alive. It has neither fears nor anxieties, because it is incorrigibly poetical. It idealizes everything that it

6

touches. It is unfair, perhaps, to blame parents and teachers, as we sometimes do in youth, for consciously biasing our child-minds in a falsely idealistic direction; for the child will infallibly idealize even his poorest of experiences. His broken glimpses and anticipations of his own future show him everything that is orderly, happy, and beautifully fit. He sees his grown-up life as old age, itself a sort of reversed childhood, sees its youth. The passing of childhood into youth is, therefore, like suddenly being turned from the cosy comfort of a warm fireside to shift for one's self in the world. Life becomes in a moment a process of seeking and searching. It appears as a series of blind alleys, all equally and magnificently alluring, all equally real and possible. Youth's thirst for experience is simply that it wants to be everything, do everything and have everything that is presented to its imagination. Youth has suddenly become conscious of life. It has eaten of the tree of the knowledge of good and evil.

As the world breaks in on a boy with its crashing thunder, he has a feeling of expansion, of sudden wisdom and sudden care. The atoms of things seem to be disintegrating around him. Then come the tearings and the grindings and the wrenchings, and in that conflict the radical or the poet is made. If the youth takes the struggle easily, or if his guardian angels have arranged things so that there is no struggle, then he becomes of that conservative stripe that we have renounced above. But if he takes it hard, — if his struggles are not only with outward material conditions, but also with inner spiritual ones, — then he is likely to achieve that gift of the gods, perpetual youth. The great paradox is that it is the sleek and easy who are prematurely and permanently old. Struggle brings youth rather than old age.

In this struggle, thus beset with problems and crises, all calling for immediate solution, youth battles its way into a sort of rationalization. Out of its inchoateness emerges a sort of order; the disturbing currents of impulse are gradually resolved into a character. But it is essential that that resolution be a natural and not a forced one. I always have a suspicion of boys who talk of "planning their lives." I feel that they have won a precocious maturity in some illegitimate way. For to most of us youth is so imperious that those who can escape the hurly-burly and make a sudden leap into the prudent, quiet waters of life seem to have missed youth altogether. And I do not

8

mean here the hurly-burly of passion so much as of ideals. It seems so much better, as well as more natural, to expose one's self to the full fury of the spiritual elements, keeping only one purpose in view, — to be strong and sincere, — than to pick one's way cautiously along.

The old saying is the truest philosophy of youth: "Seek ye first the Kingdom of God, and all these things shall be added unto you." How impossible for a youth who is really young to plan his life consciously! This process that one sometimes sees of cautiously becoming acquainted with various ideas and systems, and then choosing deliberately those that will be best adapted to a concerted plan, is almost uncanny. This confidence in one's immunity to ideas that would tend to disarrange the harmony of the scheme is mystifying and irritating. Youth talks of "getting" or "accepting" ideas! But youth does not get ideas, — ideas get him! He may try to keep himself in a state of spiritual health, but that is the only immunity he can rely upon. He cannot really tell what idea or appeal is going to seize upon him next and make off with him.

We speak as if falling in love were a unique phase in the life of youth. It is rather the pattern

9

and symbol of a youth's whole life. This sudden, irresistible seizure of enthusiasm that he cannot explain, that he does not want to explain, what is it but the aspect of all his experience? The youth sees a pretty face, reads a noble book, hears a stirring appeal for a cause, meets a charming friend, gets fired with the concept of science, or of social progress, becomes attracted to a profession, — the emotion that fixes his enthusiasm and lets out a flood of emotion in that direction, and lifts him into another world, is the same in every case. Youth glories in the sudden servitude, is content to let the new master lead wherever he will; and is as surprised as any one at the momentous and startling results. Youth is vulnerable at every point. Prudence is really a hateful thing in youth. A prudent youth is prematurely old. It is infinitely better, I repeat, for a boy to start ahead in life in a spirit of moral adventure, trusting for sustenance to what he may find by the wayside, than to lay in laboriously, before starting, a stock of principles for life, and burden himself so heavily for the journey that he dare not, and indeed cannot, leave his pack unguarded by the roadside to survey the fair prospects on either hand. Youth at its best is this constant susceptibility to the new, this constant eagerness to try experiments.

It is here that youth's quarrel with the elder generation comes in. There is no scorn so fierce as that of youth for the inertia of older men. The lack of adjustment to the ideas of youth's elders and betters, one of the permanent tragedies of life, is certainly the most sensational aspect of youth. That the inertia of the older people is wisdom, and not impotence, is a theory that you will never induce youth to believe for an instant. The stupidity and cruelties of their management of the world fill youth with an intolerant rage. In every contact with its elders, youth finds them saying, in the words of Kipling: —

" We shall not acknowledge that old stars fade and alien
    planets arise,
That the sere bush buds or the desert blooms or the
    ancient well-head dries,
Or any new compass wherewith new men adventure
    'neath new skies."

Youth sees with almost a passionate despair its plans and dreams and enthusiasms, that it knows so well to be right and true and noble, brushed calmly aside, not because of any sincere searching into their practicability, but because

11

of the timidity and laziness of the old, who sit in the saddle and ride mankind. And nothing torments youth so much as to have this inertia justified on the ground of experience. For youth thinks that it sees through this sophism of "experience." It sees in it an all-inclusive attempt to give the world a character, and excuse the older generation for the mistakes and failures which it has made. What is this experience, youth asks, but a slow accretion of inhibitions, a learning, at its best, not to do again something which ought not to have been done in the first place?

Old men cherish a fond delusion that there is something mystically valuable in mere quantity of experience. Now the fact is, of course, that it is the young people who have all the really valuable experience. It is they who have constantly to face new situations, to react constantly to new aspects of life, who are getting the whole beauty and terror and cruelty of the world in its fresh and undiluted purity. It is only the interpretation of this first collision with life that is worth anything. For the weakness of experience is that it so soon gets stereotyped; without new situations and crises it becomes so conventional as to be practically unconscious. Very few people get any really

12

new experience after they are twenty-five, unless there is a real change of environment. Most older men live only in the experience of their youthful years.

If we get few ideas after we are twenty-five, we get few ideals after we are twenty. A man's spiritual fabric is woven by that time, and his "experience," if he keeps true to himself, consists simply in broadening and enriching it, but not in adding to it in arithmetical proportion as the years roll on, in the way that the wise teachers of youth would have us believe.

But few men remain quite true to themselves. As their youthful ideals come into contact with the harshnesses of life, the brightest succumb and go to the wall. And the hardy ones that survive contain all that is vital in the future experience of the man, — so that the ideas of older men seem often the curious parodies or even burlesques of what must have been the cleaner and more potent ideas of their youth. Older people seem often to be resting on their oars, drifting on the spiritual current that youth has set going in life, or "coasting" on the momentum that the strong push of youth has given them.

There is no great gulf between youth and middle

13

age, as there is between childhood and youth. Adults are little more than grown-up children. This is what makes their arrogance so insulting, — the assumption that they have acquired any impartiality or objectivity of outlook, and have any better standards for judging life. Their ideas are wrong, and grow progressively more wrong as they become older. Youth, therefore, has no right to be humble. The ideals it forms will be the highest it will ever have, the insight the clearest, the ideas the most stimulating. The best that it can hope to do is to conserve those resources, and keep its flame of imagination and daring bright.

Therefore, it is perhaps unfair to say that the older generation rules the world. Youth rules the world, but only when it is no longer young. It is a tarnished, travestied youth that is in the saddle in the person of middle age. Old age lives in the delusion that it has improved and rationalized its youthful ideas by experience and stored-up wisdom, when all it has done is to damage them more or less — usually more. And the tragedy of life is that the world is run by these damaged ideals. That is why our ideas are always a generation behind our actual social conditions. Press, pulpit, and bar teem with the radicalisms of

14

thirty years ago. The dead hand of opinions formed in their college days clutches our leaders and directs their activities in this new and strangely altered physical and spiritual environment. Hence grievous friction, maladjustment, social war. And the faster society moves, the more terrific is the divergence between what is actually going on and what public opinion thinks is actually going on. It is only the young who are actually contemporaneous; they interpret what they see freshly and without prejudice; their vision is always the truest, and their interpretation always the justest.

Youth does not simply repeat the errors and delusions of the past, as the elder generation with a tolerant cynicism likes to think; it is ever laying the foundations for the future. What it thinks so wildly now will be orthodox gospel thirty years hence. The ideas of the young are the living, the potential ideas; those of the old, the dying, or the already dead. This is why it behooves youth to be not less radical, but even more radical, than it would naturally be. It must be not simply contemporaneous, but a generation ahead of the times, so that when it comes into control of the world, it will be precisely right and coincident with the conditions of the world as it finds them.

If the youth of to-day could really achieve this miracle, they would have found the secret of "perpetual youth."

In this conflict between youth and its elders, youth is the incarnation of reason pitted against the rigidity of tradition. Youth puts the remorseless questions to everything that is old and established, — Why ? What is this thing good for ? And when it gets the mumbled, evasive answers of the defenders, it applies its own fresh, clean spirit of reason to institutions, customs, and ideas, and, finding them stupid, inane, or poisonous, turns instinctively to overthrow them and build in their place the things with which its visions teem.

"This constant return to purely logical activity with each generation keeps the world supplied with visionaries and reformers, that is to say, with saviors and leaders. New movements are born in young minds, and lack of experience enables youth eternally to recall civilization to sound bases. The passing generation smiles and cracks its weather-worn jokes about youthful effusions: but this new, ever-hopeful, ever-daring, ever-doing, youthful enthusiasm, ever returning to the logical bases of religion, ethics, politics, business,

16

art, and social life, — this is the salvation of the world." [1]

This was the youthful radicalism of Jesus, and his words sound across the ages "calling civilization ever back to sound bases." With him, youth eternally reproaches the ruling generation, — "O ye of little faith!" There is so much to be done in the world; so much could be done if you would only dare! You seem to be doing so little to cure the waste and the muddle and the lethargy all around you. Don't you really care, or are you only faint-hearted? If you do not care, it must be because you do not know; let us point out to you the shockingness of exploitation, and the crass waste of human personality all around you in this modern world. And if you are faint-hearted, we will supply the needed daring and courage, and lead you straight to the attack.

These are the questions and challenges that the youth puts to his elders, and it is their shifty evasions and quibblings that confound and dishearten him. He becomes intolerant, and can see all classes in no other light than that of accomplices in a great crime. If they only knew! Swept along himself in an irrationality of energy, he does not

[1] Earl Barnes.

see the small part that reason plays in the intricate social life, and only gradually does he come to view life as a "various and splendid disorder of forces," and exonerate weak human nature from some of its heavy responsibility. But this insight brings him to appreciate and almost to reverence the forces of science and conscious social progress that are grappling with that disorder, and seeking to tame it.

Youth is the leaven that keeps all these questioning, testing attitudes fermenting in the world. If it were not for this troublesome activity of youth, with its hatred of sophisms and glosses, its insistence on things as they are, society would die from sheer decay. It is the policy of the older generation as it gets adjusted to the world to hide away the unpleasant things where it can, or preserve a conspiracy of silence and an elaborate pretense that they do not exist. But meanwhile the sores go on festering just the same. Youth is the drastic antiseptic. It will not let its elders cry peace, where there is no peace. Its fierce sarcasms keep issues alive in the world until they are settled right. It drags skeletons from closets and insists that they be explained. No wonder the older generation fears and distrusts the younger.

18

YOUTH

Youth is the avenging Nemesis on its trail. "It is young men who provide the logic, decision, and enthusiasm necessary to relieve society of the crushing burden that each generation seeks to roll upon the shoulders of the next."

Our elders are always optimistic in their views of the present, pessimistic in their views of the future; youth is pessimistic toward the present and gloriously hopeful for the future. And it is this hope which is the lever of progress, — one might say, the only lever of progress. The lack of confidence which the ruling generation feels in the future leads to that distrust of the machinery of social reform and social organization, or the use of means for ends, which is so characteristic of it to-day. Youth is disgusted with such sentimentality. It can never understand that curious paralysis which seizes upon its elders in the face of urgent social innovations; that refusal to make use of a perfectly definite programme or administrative scheme which has worked elsewhere. Youth concludes that its elders discountenance the machinery, the means, because they do not really believe in the end, and adds another count to the indictment.

Youth's attitude is really the scientific attitude.

Do not be afraid to make experiments, it says. You cannot tell how anything will work until you have tried it. Suppose science confined its interests to those things that have been tried and tested in the world, how far should we get? It is possible indeed that your experiments may produce by accident a social explosion, but we do not give up chemistry becàuse occasionally a wrong mixture of chemicals blows up a scientist in a laboratory, or medical research because an investigator contracts the disease he is fighting. The whole philosophy of youth is summed up in the word, Dare! Take chances and you will attain! The world has nothing to lose but its chains — and its own soul to gain!

I have dwelt too long on the conflicts of youth. For it has also its still places, where it becomes introspective and thinks about its destiny and the meaning of its life. In our artificial civilization many young people at twenty-five are still on the threshold of activity. As one looks back, then, over eight or nine years, one sees a panorama of seemingly formidable length. So many crises, so many startling surprises, so many vivid joys and harrowing humiliations and disappointments, that one feels startlingly old; one wonders if one will ever feel so old again. And in a sense, youth at twenty-five is older than it will ever be again. For if time is simply a succession of incidents in our memory, we seem to have an eternity behind us. Middle-aged people feel no such appalling stretch of time behind them. The years fade out one by one; often the pressure of life leaves nothing of reality or value but the present moment. Some of youth's elders seem to enjoy almost a new babyhood, while youth has constantly with it in all its vividness and multifariousness that specious wealth of abrupt changes, climaxes and disillusions that have crowded the short space of its life.

We often envy the sunny noon of the thirties and forties. These elders of ours change so little that they seem to enjoy an endless summer of immortality. They are so placid, so robust, so solidly placed in life, seemingly so much further from dissolution than we. Youth seems curiously fragile. Perhaps it is because all beauty has something of the precarious and fleeting about it. A beautiful girl seems too delicate and fine to weather a long life; she must be burning away too fast. This wistfulness and haunting pathos of life is very real to

21

youth. It feels the rush of time past it. Only youth can sing of the passing glory of life, and then only in its full tide. The older people's lament for the vanished days of youth may be orthodox, but it rings hollow. For our greatest fears are those of presentiment, and youth is haunted not only by the feeling of past change, but by the presentiment of future change.

Middle age has passed the waters; it has become static and placid. Its wistfulness for youth is unreal, and a forced sentimentality. In the same breath that it cries for its youth it mocks at youth's preoccupation with the thought of death. The lugubrious harmonies of young poets are a favorite joke. But the feeling of the precariousness of life gives the young man an intimate sense of its preciousness; nothing shocks him quite so much as that it should be ruthlessly and instantly snatched away. Middle age has acclimated itself to the earth, has settled down familiarly in it, and is easily befooled into thinking that it will live here forever, just as, when we are settled comfortably in a house, we cannot conceive ourselves as ever being dislodged. But youth takes a long time to get acclimated. It has seen so many mysteries and dangers about it, that the presence of the

YOUTH

Greatest Mystery and the Greatest Danger must be the most portentous of things to it.

It is this sense of the preciousness of his life, perhaps, that makes a youth so impatient of discipline. Youth can never think of itself as anything but master of things. Its visions are a curious blend of devotion and egotism. Its enthusiasm for a noble cause is apt to be all mixed up with a picture of itself leading the cohorts to victory. The youth never sees himself as a soldier in the ranks, but as the leader, bringing in some long-awaited change by a brilliant *coup d'état,* or writing and speaking words of fire that win a million hearts at a stroke. And he fights shy of discipline in smaller matters. He does not submit willingly to a course of work that is not immediately appealing, even for the sake of the glorious final achievement. Fortunate it is for the young man, perhaps, that there are so many organs of coercion all ready in the world for him, — economic need, tradition, and subtle influence of family ambition, — to seize him and nail him fast to some profession or trade or activity, before he is aware, or has time to protest or draw back!

It is another paradox of youth that, with all its fine enthusiasm, it should accomplish so little.

But this seeming aimlessness of purpose is the natural result of that deadly fear of having one's wings clipped by discipline. Infinitely finer, it seems to youth, is it to soar freely in the air, than to run on a track along the ground! And perhaps youth is right. In his intellectual life, the young man's scorn for the pedantic and conventional amounts almost to an obsession. It is only the men of imagination and inspiration that he will follow at all. But most of these professors, these lawyers, these preachers, — what has been their training and education, he says, but a gradual losing of the grip of life, a slow withdrawing into an ideal world of phrases and concepts and artificial attitudes? Their thought seems like the endless spinning out of a spider's web, or like the camel living upon the fat of his own hump. The youth fears this sophistication of thought as he would fear losing his soul. And this seeming perversity toward discipline is often simply his refusal to let a system submerge his own real and direct reactions to his observation and experience.

And yet as he studies more and more, and acquires a richer material for thought, a familiarity with words, and a skill in handling them, he can see the insidious temptation that comes to thinking men to move all their spiritual baggage over into that fascinating unreal world. And he admires almost with reverence the men who have been able to break through the terrible crust, and have got their thinking into close touch with life again; or, best of all, those who have kept their thinking constantly checked up with life, and are occupied with interpreting what they see about them. Youth will never be able to see that this is not the only true and right business of thought.

It is the glory of the present age that in it one can be young. Our times give no check to the radical tendencies of youth. On the contrary, they give the directest stimulation. A muddle of a world and a wide outlook combine to inspire us to the bravest of radicalisms. Great issues have been born in the last century, and are now loose in the world. There is a radical philosophy that illuminates our environment, gives us terms in which to express what we see, and coördinates our otherwise aimless reactions.

In this country, it is true, where a certain modicum of free institutions, and a certain specious enfranchisement of the human spirit have been achieved, youth may be blinded and drugged into an acquiescence in conditions, and its enthusiasm

25

may easily run into a glorification of the present. In the face of the more urgent ideals that are with us, it may be inspired by vague ideas of "liberty," or "the rights of man," and fancy it is truly radical when it is but living on the radicalisms of the past. Our political thought moves so slowly here that even our radicalism is traditional. We breathe in with the air about us the belief that we have attained perfection, and we do not examine things with our own eyes.

But more and more of the clear-sighted youth are coming to see the appalling array of things that still need to be done. The radical young man of to-day has no excuse for veering round to the conservative standpoint. Cynicism cannot touch him. For it is the beauty of the modern radical philosophy that the worse the world treats a man, the more it convinces him of the truth of his radical interpretation of it. Disillusion comes, not through hard blows, but by the insidious sappings of worldly success. And there never was a time when there were so many radical young people who cared little about that worldly success.

The secret of life is then that this fine youthful spirit should never be lost. Out of the turbulence of youth should come this fine precipitate — a sane, strong, aggressive spirit of daring and doing. It must be a flexible, growing spirit, with a hospitality to new ideas, and a keen insight into experience. To keep one's reactions warm and true, is to have found the secret of perpetual youth, and perpetual youth is salvation.

II

THE TWO GENERATIONS

II

THE TWO GENERATIONS

I⊤ is always interesting to see ourselves through the eyes of others, even though that view may be most unflattering. The recent "Letter to the Rising Generation," [1] if I may judge from the well-thumbed and underscored copy of the "Atlantic" which I picked up in the College Library, has been read with keen interest by many of my fellows, and doubtless, too, with a more emphatic approval, by our elders. The indictment of an entire generation must at its best be a difficult task, but the author of the article has performed it with considerable circumspection, skirting warily the vague and the abstract, and passing from the judge's bench to the pulpit with a facility that indicates that justice is to be tempered with mercy. The rather appalling picture which she draws of past generations holding their breath to see what my contemporaries will make of themselves suggests, too, that we are still on probation, and so, before final judgment is passed, it may be pertin-

[1] *The Atlantic Monthly*, February, 1911.

ent to attempt, if not, from the hopeless nature of the case, a defense, at least an extenuation of ourselves.

The writer's charge is pretty definite. It is to the effect that the rising generation, in its reaction upon life and the splendid world which has been handed down to it, shows a distinct softening of human fibre, spiritual, intellectual, and physical, in comparison with the generations which have preceded it. The most obvious retort to this is, of course, that the world in which we find ourselves is in no way of our own making, so that if our reactions to it are unsatisfactory, or our rebellious attitude toward it distressing, it is at least a plausible assumption that the world itself, despite the responsible care which the passing generation bestowed upon it, may be partly to blame.

But this, after all, is only begging the question. The author herself admits that we are the victims of educational experiments, and, in any event, each generation is equally guiltless of its world. We recognize with her that the complexity of the world we face only makes more necessary our bracing up for the fray. Her charge that we are not doing this overlooks, however, certain aspects

32

of the situation which go far to explain our seemingly deplorable qualities.

The most obvious fact which presents itself in this connection is that the rising generation has practically brought itself up. School discipline, since the abolition of corporal punishment, has become almost nominal; church discipline practically nil; and even home discipline, although retaining the forms, is but an empty shell. The modern child from the age of ten is almost his own master. The helplessness of the modern parent face to face with these conditions is amusing. What generation but the one to which our critic belongs could have conceived of "mothers' clubs" conducted by the public schools, in order to teach mothers how to bring up their children! The modern parent has become a sort of *parlement* registering the decrees of a Grand Monarque, and occasionally protesting, though usually without effect, against a particularly drastic edict.

I do not use this assertion as a text for an indictment of the preceding generation; I am concerned, like our critic, only with results. These are a peculiarly headstrong and individualistic character among the young people, and a complete bewilderment on the part of the parents.

33

The latter frankly do not understand their children, and their lack of understanding and of control over them means a lack of the moral guidance which, it has always been assumed, young people need until they are safely launched in the world. The two generations misunderstand each other as they never did before. This fact is a basal one to any comprehension of the situation.

Now let us see how the rising generation brings itself up. It is perfectly true that the present-day secondary education, that curious fragmentary relic of a vitally humanistic age, does not appeal to them. They will tell you frankly that they do not see any use in it. Having brought themselves up, they judge utility by their own standards, and not by those of others. Might not the fact that past generations went with avidity to their multiplication table, their Latin Grammar, and their English Bible, whereas the rising generation does not, imply that the former found some intellectual sustenance in those things which the latter fails to find? The appearance of industrial education on the field, and the desperate attempts of educational theory to make the old things palatable which fifty years ago were gulped down raw, argues, too, that there may be a grain of truth in our feeling. Only after a serious examination of our intellectual and spiritual viands should our rejection of them be attributed to a disordered condition of our stomachs.

The charge that the rising generation betrays an extraordinary love of pleasure is also true. The four years' period of high-school life among the children of the comfortable classes is, instead of being a preparation for life, literally one round of social gayety. But it is not likely that this is because former generations were less eager for pleasure, but rather because they were more rigidly repressed by parents and custom, while their energy was directed into other channels, religious, for instance. But now, with every barrier removed, we have the unique spectacle of a youthful society where there is perfectly free intercourse, an unforced social life of equals, in which there are bound to develop educative influences of profound significance. Social virtues will be learned better in such a society than they can ever be from moral precepts. An important result of this camaraderie is that the boy's and the girl's attitude toward life, their spiritual outlook, has come to be the same. The line between the two "spheres" has long disappeared in the industrial classes; it is now beginning to fade among the comfortable classes.

Our critic has not seen that this avidity for pleasure is a natural ebullition which, flaring up naturally, within a few years as naturally subsides. It goes, too, without that ennui of over-stimulation; and the fact that it has been will relieve us of the rising generation from feeling that envy which invariably creeps into the tone of the passing generation when they say, "We did not go such a pace when we were young." After this period of pleasure has begun to subside, there ensues for those who have not been prematurely forced into industry, a strange longing for independence. This feeling is most striking among the girls of the rising generation, and crops up in the most unexpected places, in families in the easiest circumstances, where to the preceding generation the idea of caring to do anything except stay at home and get married, if possible, would have been inconceivable. They want somehow to feel that they are standing on their own feet. Like their brothers, they begin to chafe under the tutelage, nominal though it is, of the home. As a result, these daughters of the comfortable classes go into trained nursing, an occupation which twenty years ago was deemed hardly respectable; or study music, or do settlement work, or even public-school teaching. Of course, girls who have had to earn their own living have long done these things; the significant point is that the late rapid increase in these professions comes from those who have a comfortable niche in society all prepared for them. I do not argue that this proves any superior quality of character on the part of this generation, but it does at least fail to suggest a desire to lead lives of ignoble sloth.

The undergraduate feels this spirit, too. He often finds himself vaguely dissatisfied with what he has acquired, and yet does not quite know what else would have been better for him. He stands on the threshold of a career, with a feeling of boundless possibility, and yet often without a decided bent toward any particular thing. One could do almost anything were one given the opportunity, and yet, after all, just what shall one do? Our critics have some very hard things to say about this attitude. They attribute it to an egotistic philosophy, imperfectly absorbed. But may it not rather be the result of that absence of repression in our bringing-up, of that rigid moulding which made our grandfathers what they were?

It must be remembered that we of the rising generation have to work this problem out alone. Pastors, teachers, and parents flutter aimlessly about with their ready-made formulas, but somehow these are less efficacious than they used to be. I doubt if any generation was ever thrown quite so completely on its own resources as ours is. Through it all, the youth as well as the girl feels that he wants to count for something in life. His attitude, which seems so egotistical to his elders, is the result of this and of a certain expansive outlook, rather than of any love of vainglory. He has never known what it was to be moulded, and he shrinks a little perhaps from going through that process. The traditional professions have lost some of their automatic appeal. They do conventionalize, and furthermore, the youth, looking at many of their representatives, the men who "count" in the world to-day, may be pardoned if he feels sometimes as if he did not want to count in just that way. The youth "who would not take special training because it would interfere with his sacred individuality" is an unfair caricature of this weighing, testing attitude toward the professions. The elder generation should remember that life is no longer the charted sea that it was to our grandfathers, and be accordingly lenient with us of the rising generation.

Business, to the youth standing on the threshold of life, presents a similar dilemma. Too often it seems like a choice between the routine of a mammoth impersonal corporation and chicanery of one kind or another, or the living by one's wits within the pale of honesty. The predatory individualist, the "hard-as-nails" specimen, does exist, of course, but we are justified in ignoring him here; for, however much his tribe may increase, it is certain that it will not be his kind, but the more spiritually sensitive, the amorphous ones of the generation, who will impress some definite character upon the age, and ultimately count for good or evil, as a social force. With these latter, it should be noted that, although this is regarded as a mercenary age, the question of gain, to an increasingly large number, has little to do with the final decision.

The economic situation in which we find ourselves, and to which not only the free, of whom we have been speaking, but also the unfree of the rising generation are obliged to react, is perhaps the biggest factor in explaining our character. In this reaction the rising generation has a very real feeling of coming straight up against a wall of diminishing opportunity. I do not see how it can be denied that practical opportunity is less for this generation than it has been for those preceding it. The man of fifty years ago, if he was intellectually inclined, was able to get his professional training at small expense, and usually under the personal guidance of his elders; if commercially inclined, he could go into a small, settled, self-respecting business house, practically a profession in itself and a real school of character. If he had a broader outlook, there was the developing West for him, or the growing industrialism of the East. It looks, at least from this distance, as if opportunity were easy for that generation. They had the double advantage of being more circumscribed in their outlook, and of possessing more ready opportunity at hand.

But these times have passed forever. Nowadays, professional training is lengthy and expensive; independent business requires big capital for success; and there is no more West. It is still as true as ever that the exceptional man will always "get there," but now it is likely to be only the exceptional man, whereas formerly all the able "got there," too. The only choice for the vast majority of the young men of to-day is between being swallowed up in the routine of a big corporation, and experiencing the vicissitudes of a small business, which is now an uncertain, rickety affair, usually living by its wits, in the hands of men who are forced to subordinate everything to self-preservation, and in which the employee's livelihood is in constant jeopardy. The growing consciousness of this situation explains many of the peculiar characteristics of our generation.

It has a direct bearing on the question of responsibility. Is it not sound doctrine that one becomes responsible only by being made responsible for something? Now, what incentive to responsibility is produced by the industrial life of to-day? In the small business there is the frank struggle for gain between employer and employee, a contest of profits *vs.* wages, each trying to get the utmost possible out of the other. The only kind of responsibility that this can possibly breed is the responsibility for one's own subsistence. In the big business, the employee is simply a small part of a big machine; his work counts for so little that he can rarely be made to feel any intimate responsibility for it.

Then, too, our haphazard industrial system

offers such magnificent opportunities to a young man to get into the wrong place. He is forced by necessity to go early, without the least training or interest, into the first work that offers itself. The dull, specialized routine of the modern shop or office, so different from the varied work and the personal touch which created interest in the past, is the last thing on earth that will mould character or produce responsibility. When the situation with an incentive appears, however, we are as ready as any generation, I believe, to meet it.

I have seen too many young men, of the usual futile bringing-up and negligible training, drift idly about from one "job" to another, without apparent ambition, until something happened to be presented to them which had a spark of individuality about it, whereupon they faced about and threw themselves into the task with an energy that brought success and honor, — I have seen too much of this not to wonder, somewhat impiously perhaps, whether this boasted character of our fathers was not rather the result of their coming into contact with the proper stimulus at the proper time, than of any tougher, grittier strain in their spiritual fibre. Those among our elders, who, deploring Socialism, insist so strenuously on the imperfections of human nature, ought not to find fault with the theory that frail humanity is under the necessity of receiving the proper stimulus before developing a good character or becoming responsible.

Nor is the rising generation any the less capable of effort when conditions call it forth. I wonder how our critic accounts for the correspondence schools which have sprung up so abundantly within the past fifteen years. They are patronized by large numbers of young men and women who have had little academic training and have gone early into industry. It is true that the students do not spend their time on the Latin grammar; they devote themselves to some kind of technical course which they have been led to believe will qualify them for a better position. But the fact that they are thus willing to devote their spare time to study certainly does not indicate a lack of effort. Rather, it is the hardest kind of effort, for it is directed toward no immediate end, and, more than that, it is superimposed on the ordinary work, which is usually quite arduous enough to fatigue the youth.

Young apprentices in any branch where there is some kind of technical or artistic appeal, such as mechanics or architecture, show an almost incredible capacity of effort, often spending, as I have seen them do, whole days over problems. I know too a young man who, appointed very young to political office, found that the law would be useful to him, and travels every evening to a near-by city to take courses. His previous career had been most inglorious, well calculated by its aimlessness to ruin any "character"; but the incentive was applied, and he proved quite capable of putting forth a surprising amount of steady effort.

Our critics are perhaps misled by the fact that these young men do not announce with a blare of trumpets that they are about to follow in the footsteps of an Edison or a Webster. It must be admitted that even such men as I have cited do still contrive to work into their time a surprising amount of pleasure. But the whole situation shows conclusively, I think, that our author has missed the point when she says that the rising generation shows a real softening of the human fibre. It is rather that we have the same reserves of ability and effort, but that from the complex nature of the economic situation these reserves are not unlocked so early or so automatically as with former generations.

THE TWO GENERATIONS

The fact that our fathers did not need correspondence schools or night schools, or such things, implies either that they were not so anxious as we to count in the world, or that success was an easier matter in their day, either of which conclusions furnishes a pretty good extenuation of our apparent incapacity. We cannot but believe that our difficulties are greater in this generation; it is hard to see that the effort we put forth to overcome these difficulties is not proportional to that increase. I am aware that to blame your surroundings when the fault lies in your own character is the one impiety which rouses the horror of present-day moral teachers. Can it not count to us for good, then, that most of us, while coming theoretically to believe that this economic situation explains so much of our trouble, yet continue to act as if our deficiencies were all our own fault?

Our critics are misled by the fact that we do not talk about unselfishness and self-sacrifice and duty, as their generation apparently used to do, and conclude that we do not know what these things mean. It is true that we do not fuss and fume about our souls, or tend our characters like a hot-house plant. This is a changing, transi-

45

tional age, and our view is outward rather than inward. In an age of newspapers, free libraries, and cheap magazines, we necessarily get a broader horizon than the passing generation had. We see what is going on in the world, and we get the clash of different points of view, to an extent which was impossible to our fathers. We cannot be blamed for acquiring a suspicion of ideals, which, however powerful their appeal once was, seem singularly impotent now, or if we seek for motive forces to replace them, or for new terms in which to restate the world. We have an eagerness to understand the world in which we live that amounts almost to a passion. We want to get behind the scenes, to see how the machinery of the modern world actually works. We are curious to learn what other people are thinking, and to get at the forces that have produced their point of view. We dabble in philanthrophy as much from curiosity to see how people live as from any feeling of altruism. We read all sorts of strange philosophies to get the personal testimony of men who are interpreting the world. In the last analysis, we have a passion to understand why people act as they do.

We have, as a result, become impatient with the

conventional explanations of the older generation. We have retained from childhood the propensity to see through things, and to tell the truth with startling frankness. This must, of course, be very disconcerting to a generation, so much of whose activity seems to consist in glossing over the unpleasant things or hiding the blemishes on the fair face of civilization. There are too many issues evaded which we would like to meet. Many of us find, sooner or later, that the world is a very different sort of place from what our carefully deodorized and idealized education would have us believe.

When we find things simply not as they are painted, is it any wonder that we turn to the new prophets rather than to the old? We are more than half confident that the elder generation does not itself really believe all the conventional ideals which it seeks to force upon us, and much of our presumption is a result of the contempt we naturally feel for such timorousness. Too many of your preachers seem to be whistling simply to keep up your courage. The plain truth is that the younger generation is acquiring a positive faith, in contact with which the elder generation with its nerveless negations feels its helplessness with-

out knowing just what to do about it except to
scold the young.

This positive aspect is particularly noticeable
in the religion of the rising generation. As our
critic says, the religious thinking of the preceding
generation was destructive and uncertain. We
are demanding a definite faith, and our spiritual
centre is rapidly shifting from the personal to the
social in religion. Not personal salvation, but
social; not our own characters, but the character
of society, is our interest and concern. We feel
social injustice as our fathers felt personal sin.
Settlement work and socialist propaganda, things
done fifty years ago only by rare and heroic souls
like Kingsley, Ruskin, and Maurice, are now the
commonplaces of the undergraduate.

The religion that will mean anything to the
rising generation will be based on social ideals. An
essay like ex-President Eliot's "Religion of the
Future," which in a way synthesizes science and
history and these social ideals and gives them the
religious tinge which every age demands, supplies
a real working religious platform to many a young
man and woman of the rising generation, and an
inspiration of which our elders can form no conception. Perhaps it is unfair to call this religion

48

at all. Perhaps it is simply the scientific attitude toward the world. But I am sure that it is more than this; I am sure that it is the scientific attitude tinged with the religious that will be ours of the rising generation. We find that we cannot keep apart our religion, our knowledge, our practice, and our hopes in water-tight compartments, as our ancestors did. We are beginning to show an incorrigible tendency to work our spiritual assimilations into one intelligible, constructive whole.

It is to this attitude rather than to a softening of fibre that I think we may lay our growing disinclination to deify sacrifice and suffering. A young chemistry student said to me the other day, "Science means that nothing must be wasted!" This idea somehow gets mixed up with human experience, and we come to believe that human life and happiness are things that must not be wasted. Might it not be that such a belief that human waste of life and happiness was foolish and unnecessary would possibly be of some avail in causing that waste to disappear? And one of the most inspiring of the prophets to the rising generation, William James, has told us that certain "moral equivalents" of these things are possible which will prevent that incurable decaying of fibre which the elder generation so anxiously, fears.

Another result of this attitude is our growing belief in political machinery. We are demanding of our preachers that they reduce quality to quantity. "Stop talking about liberty and justice and love, and show us institutions, or concerted attempts to model institutions that shall be free or just or lovely," we cry. You have been trying so long to reform the world by making men "good," and with such little success, that we may be pardoned if we turn our attention to the machinery of society, and give up for a time the attempt to make the operators of that machinery strictly moral. Indeed, the charm of Socialism to so many of the rising generation is just that scientific aspect of it, its claim of historical basis, and its very definite and concrete organization for the attainment of its ends. A philosophy which gives an illuminating interpretation of the present, and a vision of the future, with a definitely crystallized plan of action with concrete methods, however unsound it may all be, can hardly be said to appeal simply to the combination of "a weak head, a soft heart, and a desire to shirk."

THE TWO GENERATIONS

Placed in such a situation as we are, and with such an attitude toward the world, we are as interested as you and the breathless generations behind you to see what destinies we shall work out for ourselves. An unpleasantly large proportion of our energy is now drained off in fighting the fetishes which you of the elder generation have passed along to us, and which, out of some curious instinct of self-preservation, you so vigorously defend. We, on the other hand, are becoming increasingly doubtful whether you believe in yourselves quite so thoroughly as you would have us think. Your words are very brave, but the tone is hollow. Your mistrust of us, and your reluctance to convey over to us any of your authority in the world, looks a little too much like the fear and dislike that doubt always feels in the presence of conviction, to be quite convincing. We believe in ourselves; and this fact, we think, is prophetic for the future. We have an indomitable feeling that we shall attain, or if not, that we shall pave the way for a generation that shall attain.

Meanwhile our constructive work is hampered by your distrust, while you blame us for our lack of accomplishment. Is this an attitude calculated

51

to increase our responsibility and our self-respect? Would it not be better in every way, more constructive and more fruitful, to help us in our aspirations and endeavors, or, failing that, at least to strive to understand just what those aspirations and endeavors are?

III

THE VIRTUES AND THE SEASONS OF LIFE

III

THE VIRTUES AND THE SEASONS OF LIFE

EACH season of life has its proper virtues, as each season of the year has its own climate and temperature. If virtue is the excellent working of the soul, then youth, middle age, and old age, all have their peculiar ways of working excellently. When we speak of a virtuous life, we should mean, not a life that has shown one single thread of motive and attitude running through it, but rather one that has varied with the seasons, as spring grows gently into summer and summer into autumn, each season working excellently in respect to the tilling and harvest of the soul. If it is a virtue to be contented in old age, it is no virtue to be contented in youth; if it is a virtue for youth to be bold and venturesome, it is the virtue of middle life to take heed and begin to gather up the lines and nets so daringly cast by youth into the sea of life. A virtuous life means a life responsive to its powers and its opportunities, a life not of inhibitions, but of a straining up to the

55

limit of its strength. It means doing every year
what is fitting to be done at that year to enhance
or conserve one's own life or the happiness of those
around one. Virtue is a word that abolishes duty.
For duty has steadily fallen into worse and worse
opprobrium; it has come to mean nothing but
effort and stress. It implies something that is
done rightly, but that cuts straight across the
grain of all one's inclinations and motive forces.
It is following the lines of greatest resistance; it
is the working of the moral machine with the utmost friction possible. Now there is no doubt
that the moral life involves struggle and effort,
but it should be the struggle of adequate choice,
and not of painful inhibition. We are coming to
see that the most effective things we do are those
that have some idea of pleasure yoked up with
them. In the interests of moral efficiency, the
ideal must be the smooth and noiseless workings
of the machine, and not the rough and grinding
movements that we have come to associate with
the word "duty." For the emphasis on the negative duty we must substitute emphasis on the
positive virtue. For virtue is excellence of working, and all excellence is pleasing. When we know
what are the virtues appropriate to each age of

life, we can view the moral life in a new light. It becomes not a claim upon us of painful obligation, but a stimulus to excellent spontaneity and summons to self-expression.

In childhood we acquire the spiritual goods that we shall take with us through life; in youth we test our acquisitions and our tools, selecting, criticizing, comparing; in old age, we put them away gently into the attic of oblivion or retire them honorably, full of years and service. Our ideas, however, of what those spiritual goods were that childhood acquired have been very much confused. We have imagined that we could give the child "the relish of right and wrong," as Montaigne calls it. The attempt has usually been made to train up the child in the moral life, by telling him from his earliest years what was right and what was wrong. It was supposed that in this way he absorbed right principles that would be the guiding springs of his youthful and later life. The only difficulty, of course, with this theory is that the moral life hardly begins before the stresses and crises of youth at all. For really moral activity implies choice and it implies significant choice; and the choices of the child are few in number and seldom significant. You can tell a child that a certain thing is wrong, and he will believe it, but his belief will be a purely mechanical affair, an external idea, which is no more woven into the stuff of his life than is one of those curious "post-hypnotic suggestions," that psychologists tell about, where the subject while hypnotized is told to do something at a certain time after he awakes. When the time comes he does it without any consciousness of the reason and without any immediate motive. Now most moral ideas in a child's mind are exactly similar to these suggestions. They seem to operate with infallible accuracy, and we say, — "What a good child!" As a fact the poor child is as much under an alien spell as the subject of the hypnotist. Now all this sort of hypnotized morality the younger generation wants to have done with. It demands a morality that is glowing with self-consciousness, that is healthy with intelligence. It refuses to call the "good" child moral at all; it views him as a poor little trained animal, that is doomed for the rest of his life to go through mechanical motions and moral tricks at the crack of the whip of a moral code or religious authority. From home and Sunday-school, children of a slightly timid disposition get moral wounds, the scars of which never

58

heal. They enter a bondage from which they can never free themselves; their moral judgment in youth is warped and blighted in a thousand ways, and they pass through life, seemingly the most moral of men and women, but actually having never known the zest of true morality, the relish of right and wrong. The best intentions of parents and teachers have turned their characters into unnatural channels from which they cannot break, and fixed unwittingly upon them senseless inhibitions and cautions which they find they cannot dissolve, even when reason and common sense convince them that they are living under an alien code. Looked upon from this light, childish goodness and childish conscientiousness is an unhealthy and even criminal forcing of the young plant, the hot-house bringing to maturity of a young soul whose sole business is to grow and learn. When moral instruction is given, a criminal advantage is taken of the child's suggestibility, and all possibility of an individual moral life, growing naturally and spontaneously as the young soul meets the real emergencies and problems that life will present to it, is lost. If, as we are coming more and more to realize, the justification of knowledge is that it helps us to get along with and enjoy and grapple with the world, so the justification of virtue is that it enables us to get along with and enjoy and grapple with the spiritual world of ideals and feelings and qualities. We should be as careful about giving a child moral ideas that will be of no practical use to him as we are in giving him learning that will be of no use to him.

The virtues of childhood, then, we shall not find in the moral realm. The "good" child is not cultivated so much to-day as he was by the former generation, whose one aim in education and religion was to bind the young fast in the fetters of a puritan code; but he is still, in well-brought-up families, an appalling phenomenon. The child, who at the age of five has a fairly complete knowledge of what God wants him and all around him to do and not to do, is an illustration of the results of the confusion of thought that would make childhood instead of youth the battle-ground of the moral life. We should not dismiss such a child as quaint, for in him have been sowed the seeds of a general obscurantism and conservatism that will spread like a palsy over his whole life. The acceptance of moral judgments that have no vital meaning to the young soul will mean in later life the acceptance of ideas and prejudices in political and religious and social matters that are uncriticized and unexamined. The "good" child grows up into the conventional bigoted man. The duties and tastes which are inculcated into him in childhood, far from aiding the "excellent workings of his soul," clog and rust it, and prevent the fine free expression of its individuality and genius. For the child has not yet the material of experience that will enable him to get the sense of values which is at the bottom of what we call the spiritual life. And it is this sense that is so easily dulled, and that must be so carefully protected against blunting. That the child cannot form moral judgments for himself, however, does not mean that they must be formed for him by others; it means that we must patiently wait until he meets the world of vivid contrasts and shocks and emergencies that is youth. It is not repairing his lack of moral sensitiveness to get him to repeat parrot-like the clean-cut and easily learned taboos and permissions of the people around him. To get him to do this is exactly like training an animal to bolt any kind of food. The child, however, has too weak a stomach to digest very much of the moral pabulum that is fed him. The inevitable result is a moral indigestion, one form of which is the once fashionable sense of sin. The youth, crammed with uncriticized taboos delivered to him with the awful prestige of an Almighty God, at a certain age revolts, and all the healthy values of life turn sour within him. The cure for this spiritual dyspepsia is called conversion, but it is a question whether the cure is not often worse than the disease. For it usually means that the relish of right and wrong, which had suddenly become a very real thing, has been permanently perverted in a certain direction. By a spiritual operation, the soul has been forced to digest all this strange food, and acquires the ability to do so forever after. Those who do not suffer this operation pass through life with an uneasiness of spirit, the weight and burden of an imperfectly assimilated moral life. Few there are who are able to throw off the whole soddenness, and if they do they are fortunate if they are not left without any food at all. Religious teachers have always believed that all these processes were necessary for the soul's health. They have believed that it was better to have mechanical morals than no morals at all. When the younger generation sees the damage such morals work, it would prefer to have none.

Discarding the "good" child, then, we will find

the virtues of childhood in that restless, pushing, growing curiosity that is the characteristic of every healthy little boy or girl. The child's life is spent in learning his way around the world; in learning the ropes of things, the handles and names of whatever comes within the range of his experience. He is busy acquiring that complex bundle of common-sense knowledge that under-lies all our grown-up acts, and which has become so automatic with us that it hardly seems possible to us that we have slowly acquired it all. We do not realize that thousands of facts and habits, which have become stereotyped and practically uncon-scious in our minds, are the fresh and vital experi-ences of the mind of the little child. We cannot put ourselves back into that world where the absorbing business is to give things a position and a name and to learn all the little obvious facts about the things in the house and the yard and the village, and in that far land of mystery be-yond. What sort of sympathy can we have with these little people, — we, to whom all this naïve world of place and nomenclature is so familiar as to seem intuitive? We should have to go back to a world where every passing railroad train was a marvel and a delight, where a walk to the village meant casting ourselves adrift into an adventurous country where anything was likely to happen and where all calculations of direction or return were upset. It takes children a long time to get accustomed to the world. This common workaday knowledge of ours seems intuitive to us only because we had so many years during which it was reiterated to us, and not because we were unusually sensitive to impressions. Children often seem almost as stupid as any young animal, and to require long practice before they know their way around in the world, although, once obtained, this common sense is never forgotten. That child is virtuous who acquires all he can of it.

This curiosity of childhood makes children the first scientists. They begin, as soon as their eyes are open, dissolving this confused mystery of the world, distinguishing and classifying its parts according to their interests and needs. They push on and on, ever widening the circle, and ever bringing more and more of their experience under the subjugation of their understanding. They begin the process that the scientist completes. As children, after several years we came to know our house and yard, although the attic and cellar were perhaps still dim and fearsome places. Inside the household things were pretty well tabulated and rationalized. It was only when we went outside the gate that we might expect adventures to happen. We should have been very much shocked to see the fire leap from the stove and the bread from the table, as they did in the "Blue Bird," but in walking down to the village we should not have been surprised to see a giant or a fairy sitting on the green. When we became familiar with the village, the fairies were, of course, banished to remoter regions, until they finally vanished altogether. But it is not so long ago that I lost the last vague vestige of a feeling that there were fairies in England.

The facility, one might almost say skill, which children show in getting lost, is the keynote of childhood's world. For they have no bearings among the unfamiliar, no principles for the solution of the unknown. In their accustomed realm they are as wise and canny and free from superstition as we are in ours. We, as grown-ups, have not acquired any magical release from fantasy. The only difference is that we are accustomed to make larger hazards of faith that things will repeat themselves, and that we have a wider experience to check off our novelties by. We have charted most of our world; we unfortunately have no longer any world to get lost in. To be sure, we have opened up perhaps an intangible world of philosophy and speculation, which childhood does not dream of, and heaven knows we can get lost there! But the thing is different. The adventure of childhood is to get lost here in this every-day world of common sense which is so familiar to us. To become really as little children we should have to get lost again here. The best substitute we can give ourselves is to keep exploring the new spiritual world in which we may find ourselves in youth and middle life, pushing out ever, as the child does, our fringe of mystery. And we can gain the gift of wonder, something that the child does not have. He is too busy drinking in the facts to wonder about them, or to wonder about what is beyond them. We may count ourselves fortunate, however, that we are able to retain the child's virtue of curiosity, and transmute it into the beauty of spiritual wonder.

It is facts and not theories that the child is curious about, and rightly. He cannot assimilate moral theories, nor can he assimilate any other kind of theories. It is his virtue to learn how the world runs; youth will be time enough to philosophize about that running. It is the immediate and the present that interest children, and they are omnivorous with regard to any facts about either. What they hear about the world they accept without question. We often think when we are telling them fairy stories or animal stories that we are exercising their poetic imagination; but from their point of view we are telling them sober facts about the world they live in. We are often surprised, too, at the apathy they show in the midst of wonders that we point out to them. They are wonders to us because we appreciate the labor or the genius that has produced them. In other words, we have added a value to them. But it is just this value which the child-mind does not get and can never get. To the child they are not surprising, but simply some more information about his world. All is grist that comes to the child's mill. Everything serves to plot and track for him a new realm of things as they are.

The child's mind, so suggestible to facts, seems to be almost impervious to what we call spiritual influences. He lives in a world hermetically sealed to our interests and concerns. Parents and teachers make the most conscientious efforts to influence their children, but they would better realize that they can influence them only in the most indirect way. The best thing they can do for the children is to feed their curiosity, and provide them with all the materials that will stimulate their varied interests. They can then leave the "influence" to take care of itself. The natural child seems to be impregnable to any appeals of shame, honor, reverence, honesty, and even ridicule, — in other words, to all those methods we have devised for getting a clutch on other people's souls, and influencing and controlling them according to our desires. And this is not because the child is immoral, but simply because, as I have tried to show, those social values mean as yet nothing to him. He lives in a splendid isolation from our conventional standards; the influences of his elders, however well-directed and prayerful they may be, simply do not reach him. He lives unconscious of our interests and motives. Only the "good" child is susceptible, and he is either instinctively submissive, or is the victim of the mechanical imposition of standards and moral ideas.

The child works out what little social morality he does obtain, not under the influence of his elders, but among his playmates. And the stand-

ards worked out there are not refined and moral
at all, but rough ones of emulation and group
honor, and respect for prowess. Even obedience,
which we all like to think of as one of the indispensable accomplishments of a well-trained child,
seems to be obtained at the cost of real moral
growth. It might be more beneficial if it were not
too often merely a means for the spiritual edifica-
tion of the parents themselves. Too often it is the
delight of ruling, of being made obeisance to, that
is the secret motive of imposing strict obedience,
and not our desire simply that they shall learn the
excellent habits that are our own. One difficulty
with the child who has "learned to mind" is that,
if he learns too successfully, he runs the risk of
growing up to be a cowardly and servile youth.
There is a theory that since the child will be
obliged in later life to do many things that he does
not want to do, he might as well learn how while
he is young. The difficulty here seems to be that
learning to do one kind of a thing that you do not
want to do does not guarantee your readiness to
do other kinds of unpleasant things. That art
cannot be taught. Each situation of compulsion,
unless the spirit is completely broken, will have
its own peculiar quality of bitterness, and no

guarantee against it can be inculcated. Life will present so many inevitable necessities to the child when he gets out into the world that it seems premature to burden his childhood with a training which will be largely useless. So much of our energy is wasted, and so much friction created, because we are unwilling to trust life. If life is the great demoralizer, it is also the great moralizer. It whips us into shape, and saddles us with responsibilities and the means of meeting them, with obligations and the will to meet them, with burdens and a strength to bear them. It creates in us a conscience and the love of duty, and endows us with a morality that a mother and father with the power and the love of angels working through all the years of our childhood could not have created within us. Trust life and not your own feeble efforts to create the soul in the child!

The virtue of childhood, then, is an exhaustless curiosity and interest in the world in which the child finds himself. He is here to learn his way around in it, to learn the names of things and their uses, how to use his body and his capacities. This will be the most excellent working of his soul. If his mind and body are active, he will be a "good" child, in the best sense of the word. We can almost afford to let him be insolent and irreverent and troublesome as long as he is only curious. If he has a temper, it will not be cured by curbing, but by either letting it burn out, or not giving it fuel to feed on. Food for his body and facts for his mind are the sustenance he requires. From the food will be built up his body, and from the facts and his reactions to them will slowly evolve his world of values and ideals. We cannot aid him by giving him our theories, or shorten the path for him by presenting him with ready-made standards. In spite of all the moral teachers, there is no short cut to the moral life of youth, any more than there is a royal road to knowledge. Nor can we help him to grow by transferring some of our superfluous moral flesh to his bones. The child's qualities which shock our sense of propriety are evidences not of his immorality, but of his pre-morality. A morality that will mean anything to him can only be built up out of a vast store of experience, and only when his world has broadened out into a real society with influences of every kind coming from every side. He cannot get the relish of right and wrong until he has tasted life, and it is the taste of life that the child does not have. That taste comes only with youth, and then with a bewildering complexity and vividness.

But between childhood and youth there comes a trying period when the child has become well cognizant of the practical world, but has as yet no hint of the gorgeous colors of youth. At thirteen, for instance, one has the world pretty well charted, but not yet has the slow chemistry of time transmuted this experience into meanings and values. There is a crassness and materiality about the following three or four years that have no counterpart until youth is over and the sleek years of the forties have begun. How cocksure and familiar with the world is the boy or girl at this age! They have no doubts, but they have no glow. At no time in life is one so unspiritual, so merely animal, so much of the earth, earthy. How different is it to be a few years later! How shaken and adventurous will the world appear then! For this waiting period of life, the virtues are harder to discover. Curiosity has lapsed, for there do not seem to be many things left to be curious about. The child is beautifully unconscious of his own ignorance. Similarly has the play activity diminished; the boy has put away his Indian costumes, and the girl her dolls. At this season of life the virtue would seem to consist in the acquirement of some skill in some art or handicraft or technique. This is the time to search for the budding talents and the strong native bents and inclinations. To be interesting is one of the best of virtues, and few things make a person more interesting than skill or talent. From a selfish point of view, too, all who have grown up with unskillful hands will realize the solid virtue of knowing how to do something with the hands, and avoid that vague restlessness and desire to get at grips with something that haunts the professional man who has neglected in youth to cultivate this virtue of technique. And it is a virtue which, if not acquired at that time, can never be acquired. The deftness of hand, alertness of mind, are soon lost if they are not taken advantage of, and the child grows up helpless and unskillful, with a restless void where a talent and interest should be.

It is with youth, then, that the moral life begins, the true relish of right and wrong. Out of the crucible of passion and enthusiasm emerge the virtues of life, virtues that will have been tested and tried in the furnace of youth's poignant reactions to the world of possibilities and ideals that has been suddenly opened up to it. Those young people who have been the victims of childish morality will not feel this new world so clearly or keenly, or, if there did lurk underneath the crust of imposed priggishness some latent touch of genius, they will feel the new life with a terrible searing pain that maddens them and may permanently distort their whole vision of life. To those without the spark, the new life will come stained by prejudice. Their reactions will be dulled; they will not see clearly; and will either stagger at the shock, or go stupidly ahead oblivious of the spiritual wonders on every side. Only those who have been allowed to grow freely like young plants, with the sun and air above their heads, will get the full beauty and benefit of youth. Only those whose eyes have been kept wide open ceaselessly learning the facts of the material and practical world will truly appreciate the values of the moral world, and be able to acquire virtue. Only with this fund of practical knowledge will the youth be able to balance and contrast and compare the bits of his experience, see them in the light of their total meaning, and learn to prefer rightly one bit to another. It is as if silent forces had been at work in the soul during the last years of childhood, organizing the knowledge and nascent sentiments of the child into forms of power ready for the free expression of youth.

Youth expresses itself by falling in love. Whether it be art, a girl, socialism, religion, the sentiment is the same; the youth is swept away by a flood of love. He has learned to value, and how superlative and magnificent are his values! The little child hardly seems to love; indeed, his indifference to grown people, even to his own parents, is often amazing. He has the simple affection of a young animal, but how different his cool regard from the passionate flame of youth! Love is youth's virtue, and it is wide as well as deep. There is no tragic antithesis between a youth's devotion to a cause and his love for a girl. They are not mutually exclusive, as romanticists often love to think, but beautifully compatible. They tend to fuse, and they stimulate and ennoble each other. The first love of youth for anything is pure and ethereal and disinterested. It is only when thwarted that love turns sensual, only when mocked that enthusiasm becomes fanatical or mercenary. Worldly opinion seems to care much more for personal love than for the love of ideals. Perhaps it is instinctively more interested

75

in the perpetuation of the race than in its progress. It gives its suffrage and approval to the love of a youth for a girl, but it mocks and discredits the enthusiast. It just grudgingly permits the artist to live, but it piles almost insurmountable obstacles in the path of the young radical. The course of true love may never run smooth, but what of the course of true idealism?

The springs that feed this love are found, of course, in hero-worship. Sexual love is objectified in some charming and appealing girl, love for ideals in some teacher or seer or the inspiring personality of a friend. It is in youth that we can speak of real influence. Then is the soul responsive to currents and ideas. The embargo which kept the child's mind immune to theory and opinion and tastes is suddenly lifted. In childhood, our imitation is confined to the external; we copy ways of acting, but we are insensitive to the finer nuances of personality. But in youth we become sensitive to every passing tone and voice. Youth is the season when, through this sensitiveness, the deadly pressures get their purchase on the soul; it is also the season for the most momentous and potent influences for good. In youth, if there is the possibility that the soul be permanently

warped out of shape, there is also the possibility
that it receive the nourishment that enables it to
develop its own robust beauty. It is by hero-
worship that we copy not the externals of personality, as in childhood, but the inner spirit. We
feel ourselves somehow merged with the admired
persons, and we draw from them a new stimulating
grace. We find ourselves in them. It is not yielding to a pressure that would force us to a type,
but a drawing up of ourselves to a higher level,
through the aid of one who possesses all those
qualities which have been all along, we feel, our
vague and hitherto unexpressed ideal. We do not
feel that our individualities are being lost, but
that they are for the first time being found. We
have discovered in another personality all those
best things for which our hearts have been hun-
gering, and we are simply helping ourselves to
that which is in reality our own. Our hero gives
of himself inexhaustibly, and we take freely and
gladly what we need. It is thus that we stock up
with our first store of spiritual values. It is from
the treasury of a great and good personality that
we receive the first confirmation of ourselves. In
the hero-personality, we see our own dim, baby
ideals objectified. Their splendor encourages us,

and nerves us for the struggle to make them thoroughly our own.

There is a certain pathos in the fact that parents are so seldom the heroes from whom the children derive this revelation of their own personality. It is more often some teacher or older friend or even a poet or reformer whom the youth has never seen and knows only through his words and writings. But for this the parents are partly responsible. They are sufficiently careful about the influences which play upon their young children. They give care and prayers and tears to their bringing-up in the years when the children are almost immune to any except the more obvious mechanical influences, and learn of ideals and values only in a parrot-like fashion. But when the child approaches youth, the parent is apt to relax vigilance and, with a cry of thanksgiving and self-congratulation that the child has been brought safely through so many perils to the desired haven, to surrender him to his own devices. Just at the time when he becomes really sensitive for the first time to spiritual influences, he is deprived of this closest and warmest influence of the home. But he has not been brought into a haven, but launched into a heaving and troubled sea. This is the time when his character lies at stake, and the possibility of his being a radical, individual force in the world hangs in the balance. Whether he will become this force depends on the pressures that he is able to dodge, and on the positive ideals he is able to secure. And they will depend largely on the heroes he worships, upon his finding the personalities that seem to contain all the best for which he yearns. Hero-worship is the best preservative against cheapness of soul, that besetting sin of modern youth. It directs our attention away from the light and frothy things of the world, which are wont to claim so much of youth's interest, to qualities that are richer and more satisfying. Yet hero-worship is no mere imitation. We do not simply adopt new qualities and a new character. We rather impregnate our hitherto sterile ideals with the creative power of a tested and assured personality, and give birth to a new reliance and a new faith. Our heroes anticipate and provide for our doubts and fears, and fortify us against the sternest assaults of the world. We love our heroes because they have first loved us.

Out of this virtue of love and the clashing of its clear spirit with the hard matter of established things come the sterner virtues. From that conflict, courage is struck off as youth feels the need of keeping his flame steady and holding to his own course, regardless of obstacles or consequences. Youth needs courage, that salt of the virtues, for if youth has its false hopes, it has its false depressions. That strange melancholy, when things seem to lose their substance and the world becomes an empty shell, is the reverse shield of the elation of youth. To face and overcome it is a real test of the courage of youth. The dash and audacity, the daring and self-confidence of youth, are less fine than this simple courage of optimism. Youth needs courage, too, when its desires do not come true, when it meets suspicion or neglect, and when its growth seems inexorably checked by circumstance. In these emergencies, the youth usually plays the stoic. He feels a savage pride in the thought that circumstance can never rob him of his integrity, or bring his best self to be dependent on mere change of fortune. Such a courage is a guarantor of youth. It forms a protecting crust over life and lessens the shock of many contingencies. The only danger is that it may become too perfect a shell and harden the character. It is not well for youth to shun the battle. Courage demands exposure to assault.

And besides courage, youth needs temperance. The sins and excesses of hot-blooded youth are a byword; youth would not seem to be youth without its carnality and extravagance. It is fortunate that youth is able to expend that extravagance partly in idealism. Love is always the antidote to sensuality. And we can always, if we set ourselves resolutely to the task, transmute the lower values into higher. This, indeed, is the crucial virtue of youth, and temperance is the seal and evidence of the transmutation. Temperance in things of the flesh is ordained not through sentimental reasons, but on the best of physiological and psychological motives. Temperance is a virtue because of the evil consequences to one's self and others which follow excess of indulgence in appetite.

But this temperance does not mean quite the same thing as the rigid self-control that used to be preached. The new morality has a more positive ideal than the rigid mastery which self-control implies. We are to fix our attention more in giving our good impulses full play than in checking the bad. The theory is that if one is occupied with healthy ideas and activities, there will be no room or time for the expression of the unhealthy ones. Anything that implies an inhibition or struggle to

81

repress is a draining away into a negative channel of energy that might make for positive constructive work in the character. The repressed desires and interests are not killed, but merely checked, and they persist, with unabated vigor, in struggling to get the upper hand again. They are little weakened by lying dormant, and lurk warily below, ready to swarm up again on deck, whenever there is the smallest lapse of vigilance. But if they are neglected they gradually cease from troubling, and are killed by oblivion where they could not have been hurt by forcible repression. The mortification of the flesh seems too often simply to strengthen its pride.

In the realm of emotion, the dangers of rigid self-control are particularly evident. There are fashions in emotion as well as in dress, and it seems to have become the fashion in certain circles of youth to inhibit any emotional expression of the sincere or the serious. There is a sort of reign of terrorism which prevents personal conversation from being carried on upon any plane except one of flippancy and insincerity. Frankness of expression in regard to personal feelings and likes and dislikes is tabooed. A strange new ethics of tact has grown up which makes candor so sacrilegious a thing that its appearance in a group or between two young people of the opposite sex creates general havoc and consternation. Young people who dare to give natural expression to their feelings about each other or about their ideals and outlook on life find themselves genuinely unpopular. When this peculiar ethics works at its worst, it gives a person a pride in concealing his or her feelings on any of the vital and sincere aspects of life, the interests and admirations and tastes. But this energy, dammed up thus from expression in its natural way, overflows in a hysterical admiration for the trivial, and an unhealthy interest in the mere externals, the "safe" things, of life. Such self-control dwarfs the spirit; it results only in misunderstandings and a tragic ignorance of life. It is one of the realest of the vices of youth, for it is the parent of a host of minor ailments of the soul. It seems to do little good even to repress hatred and malice. If repressed, they keep knocking at the door of consciousness, and poison the virtues that might develop if the soul could only get rid of its load of spleen. If the character is thickly sown with impersonal interests and the positive virtues are carefully cultivated, there will be no opportunity for these hateful weeds to reach the sun and air. Virtue should actually crowd out vice, and temperance is the tool that youth finds ready to its hand. Temperance means the happy harmonizing and coördinating of the expression of one's personality; it means health, candor, sincerity, and wisdom, — knowledge of one's self and the sympathetic understanding of comrades.

Justice is a virtue which, if it be not developed in youth, has little chance of ever being developed. It depends on a peculiarly sensitive reaction to good and evil, and it is only in youth that those reactions are keen and disinterested. Real justice is always a sign of great innocence; it cannot exist' side by side with interested motives or a trace of self-seeking. And a sense of justice is hard to develop in this great industrial world where the relations of men are so out of joint and where such flaunting anomalies assail one at every turn. Yet in the midst of it all youth is still pure of heart, and it is only the pure of heart who can be just. For in youth we live in a world of clean disinterestedness. We have ambitions and desires, but not yet have we learned the devious way by which they may be realized. We have not learned how to achieve our ends by taking advantage of other people, and using them and their interests and necessities as means. We still believe in the possibility of every man's realizing himself side by side with us. In early youth, therefore, we have an instinctive and almost unconscious sense of justice. Not yet have we learned the trick of exploiting our fellow men. If we are early assailed with the reality of social disorder, and have brought home to our hearts the maladjustments of our present order, that sense of justice is transformed into a passion. This passion for social justice is one of the most splendid of the ideals of youth. It has the power of keeping alive all the other virtues; it stimulates life and gives it a new meaning and tone. It furnishes the *leit-motiv* which is so sadly lacking in many lives. And youth must find a *leit-motiv* of some kind, or its spirit perishes. This social idealism acts like a tonic upon the whole life; it keeps youth alive even after one has grown older in years.

With justice comes the virtue of democracy. We learn all too early in youth the undemocratic way of thinking, the divisions and discriminations which the society around us makes among people. But youth cannot be swept by love or fired by the passion for justice without feeling a wild disgust at everything that suggests artificial inequalities and distinctions. Democracy means a belief that people are worthy; it means trust in the good faith and the dignity of the average man. The chief reason why the average man is not now worthy of more trust, the democrat believes, is simply that he has not been trusted enough in the past. Democracy has little use for philanthropy, at least in the sense of a kindly caring for people, with the constant recognition that the person who is kind is superior to the person who is being done good to. The spirit of democracy is a much more robust humanity. It is rough and aggressive; it stands people up on their own feet, makes them take up their beds and walk. It prods them to move their own limbs and take care of themselves. It makes them strong by giving them something to do. It will have nothing more to do with the superstition of trusteeship which paralyzes now most of our institutional life. It does not believe for a minute that everybody needs guardians for most of the serious concerns of life. The great crime of the past has been that humankind has never been willing to trust itself, or men each other. We have tied ourselves up with laws and traditions, and devised a thousand ways to prevent men from being thrown on their own responsibility and cultivating their own powers. Our society has been constituted on the principle that men must be saved from themselves. We have surrounded ourselves with so many moral hedges, have imposed upon ourselves so many checks and balances, that life has been smothered. Our liberation has just begun. We are far from free, but the new spirit of democracy is the angel that will free us. No virtue is more potent for youth.

And the last of these virtues, redolent of the old Greek time, when men walked boldly, when the world was still young, and gods and nymphs not all dead, is wisdom. To be wise is simply to have blended and harmonized one's experience, to have fused it together into a "philosophy of life." Wisdom is a matter not of quantity, but of quality of experience. It means getting at the heart of it, and obtaining the same clear warm impression of its meaning that the artist does of the æsthetic idea that he is going to represent. Wisdom in youth or early middle life may be far truer than in later life. One's courage may weaken under repeated failure, one's sense of justice be dulled by contact with the wrong relations between men and classes, one's belief in democracy destroyed by the seeming failure of experiments. But this gathering cynicism does not mean the acquiring of wisdom, but the losing of it. The usefulness and practicability of these virtues of youth are not really vitiated by the struggles they have in carrying themselves through into practice; what is exhibited is merely the toughness of the old forces of prejudice and tradition, and the "pig-headedness" of the old philosophy of timorousness and distrust. True wisdom is faith in love, in justice, in democracy; youth has this faith in largest measure; therefore youth is most wise.

Middle age steals upon a youth almost before he is aware. He will recognize it at first, perhaps, by a slight paling of his enthusiasms, or by a sudden consciousness that his early interests have been submerged in the flood of routine work and family cares. The later years of youth and the early years of middle life are in truth the dangerous age, for then may be lost the virtues that were acquired in youth. Or, if not lost, many will be felt to be superfluous. There is danger that the peculiar bias of the relish of right and wrong that the virtues of youth have given one may be weakened, and the soul spread itself too thin over life. Now one of the chief virtues of middle life is

88

to conserve the values of youth, to practice in
sober earnest the virtues that came so naturally
in the enthusiasm of youth, but which take on a
different hue when exposed to what seem to be the
crass facts of the workaday world. But there is
no reason why work, ambition, the raising of a
family, should dull the essential spirit of youthful idealism. It may not be so irrepressible, so
freakish, so intolerant, but it should not be different in quality and significance. The burdens of
middle life are not a warrant for the releasing of
the spiritual obligations of youth. They do not
give one the right to look back with amused regret
to the dear follies of the past. For as soon as the
spirit of youth begins to leave the soul, that soul
begins to die. Middle-aged people are too much
inclined to speak of youth as a sort of spiritual
play. They forget that youth feels that it itself has
the serious business of life, the real crises to meet.
To youth it is middle age that seems trivial and
playful. It is after the serious work of love-mak-
ing and establishing one's self in economic independence is over that one can rest and play. Youth
has little time for that sort of recreation. In middle age, most of the problems have been solved,
the obstacles overcome. There is a slackening of

the lines, a satisfied taking of one's reward. And to youth this must always seem a tragedy, that the season of life when the powers are at their highest should be the season when they are oftener turned to material than to spiritual ends. Youth has the energy and ideals, but not the vantage-ground of prestige from which to fight for them. Middle age has the prestige and the power, but too seldom the will to use it for the furtherance of its ideals. Youth has the isolation, the independence, the disinterestedness so that it may attack any foe, but it has not the reserve force to carry that attack through. Middle age has all the reserve power necessary, but is handicapped by family obligations, by business and political ties, so that its power is rarely effective for social or individual progress.

The supreme virtue of middle age will be, then, to make this difficult fusion, — to combine devotion to one's family, to one's chosen work, with devotion to the finer idealism and impersonal aims that formed one's philosophy of youth. To keep alive through all the twistings and turnings of life's road the sense of a larger humanity that needs spiritual and material succor, of the individual spiritual life of ideal interests, is a task of

90

virtue that will tax the resources of any man or woman. Yet here lies the true virtue of middle age, —to use its splendid powers to enhance the social and individual life round one, to radiate influence that transforms and elevates. The secret of such a radiant personality seems to be that one, while mingling freely in the stress of everyday life, sees all its details in the light of larger principles, against the background of their social meaning. In other words, it is a virtue of middle life to be socially self-conscious. And this spirit is the best protector against the ravages of the tough material world. Only by this social consciousness can that toughness be softened. The image of the world the way it ought to be must never be lost sight of in the picture of the world the way it is.

This conservation of the spirit is even more necessary for the woman than for the man. The active life of the latter makes it fairly certain that he, while he may become hard and callous, will at least retain some sort of grip on the world's bigger movements. There is no such certainty for the mother. Indeed, she seems often to take a real pleasure in voluntarily offering up in sacrifice at the time of marriage what few ideal interests and tastes she has. The spectacle of the young mother devoting all her time and strength to her children and husband, and surrendering all other interests to the interests of the home, is usually considered inspiring and attractive, especially by the men. Not so attractive is she thirty years later, when, her family cares having lapsed and her children scattered, she is left high and dry in the world. If she then takes a well-earned rest, it seems a pity that that rest should be so generally futile and uninteresting. Without interests and tastes, and with no longer any useful function in society, she is relegated to the most trivial amusements and pursuits. Idle and vapid, she finds nothing to do but fritter away her time. The result is a really appalling waste of economic and social energy in middle age. Now it is the virtue of this season of life to avoid all this. The woman as well as the man must realize that her home is not bounded by the walls of the house, that it has wider implications, leading out into all the interests of the community and the state. That women of this age have not yet learned to be good mothers and good citizens at the same time, does not show that it is impossible, but that it is a virtue that requires more resolution than our morality has been willing to exhibit. The relish of right and wrong must be a relish of social right and wrong as well as of individual.

As middle age passes on into old age, however, one earns a certain right of relaxation. If there is no right to let go the sympathy for the virtues of youth and the conservation of its spirit, there comes the right to give over some of the aggressive activity. To youth belongs the practical action. At no other age is there the same impulse and daring. The virtue of later middle age is to encourage and support, rather than actively engage. It is true we have never learned this lesson. We still surrender to semi-old men the authority to govern us, think for us, act for us. We endow them with spiritual as well as practical leadership, and allow them to strip youth of its opportunities and powers. We permit them to rule not only their own but all the generations. If we could be sure that their rule meant progress, we could trust them to guide us. But, in these times at least, it seems to mean nothing so much as a last fight for a discredited undemocratic philosophy that modern youth are completely through with. From this point of view one of the virtues of this middle season of life will be the imaginative understanding of youth's purposes and radical ideals. At that age, one no longer needs the same courage to face the battles of life; they are already most of them irrevocably won or lost. There is not the same claim of temperance; the passions and ambitions are relaxed. The sense of justice and democracy will have become a habit or else they will have been forever lost. Only the need of wisdom remains, — that unworldly wisdom which mellowing years can bring, which sees through the disturbance and failure of life the truth and efficacy of youth's ideal vision.

Old age is such a triumph that it may almost be justly relieved of any burden of virtues or duties; it is so unique and beautiful that the old should be given the perfect freedom of the moral city. So splendid a victory is old age over the malign forces of disease and weakness and death that one is tempted to say that its virtue lies simply in being old. Those virtues of youth which grew out of the crises and temptations, physical and spiritual, of early life, are no longer relevant. There may come instead the quieter virtues of contentment and renunciation. Old people have few crises and few temptations; they live in the past and not in the future, as youth does. They

94

cannot be required, therefore, to have that scorn for tradition which is the virtue of youth. They can keep alive for us the tradition that *is* vital, and from them we can learn many things.

The value of their experience to us is not that it teaches us to avoid their mistakes, for we must try all things for ourselves. The older generation, it is true, often flatters itself that its mistakes somehow make for our benefit, because we learn from their errors to avoid the pitfalls into which they came. But there is no making mistakes by the proxy of a former generation. The world has moved on in the mean time; the pitfalls are new, and we shall only entangle ourselves the more by adopting the methods of our ancestors in getting out of the difficulties. But the value of an old man's experience is that he has preserved in it the living tradition and hands down to us old honesties, old sincerities, and old graces, that have been crushed in the rough-and-tumble of modern life. It is not tradition in itself that is dangerous, but only dead tradition that has no meaning for the present and is a mere weight on our progress. Such is the legal and economic tradition given to us by our raucous, middle-aged leaders of opinion, adopted by them through motives of present gain, and not through sincere love of the past.

But old men, looking back over the times in which they have lived, throw a poetic glamour over the past and make it live again. They see it idealized, but it is the *real* that they see idealized. An old man of personality and charm has the faculty of cutting away from the past the dead wood, and preserving for us the living tissue which we can graft profitably on our own growing present. Old men have much of the disinterestedness of youth; they have no ulterior motive in giving us the philosophy of their past. The wisest of them instinctively select what is vital for our present nourishment. It is not old men that youth has to fear, but the semi-old, who have lost touch with their youth, and have not lived long enough to get the disinterested vision of their idealized past. But old men who have lived this life of radical virtue are the best of teachers; they distill the perfume of the past, and bring it to us to sweeten our present. Such men grow old only in body. The radical spirit of youth has the power of abolishing considerations of age; the body changes, but the spirit remains the same. In this sense, it is the virtue of old age not to become old.

VIRTUES AND SEASONS OF LIFE

The besetting sin of this season of life is apathy. Old age should not be a mere waiting for death. The fact that we cannot reconcile death with life shows that they ought not to be discussed in the same terms. They belong to two different orders. Death has no part in life, and in life there can be no such thing as preparation for death. An old man lives to his appointed time, and then his life ends; but the life up to that ending, barring the loss of his faculties, has been all life and not a whit death. Old men do not fear death as much as do young men, and this calmness is not so much a result of disillusionment with life as a recognition that their life has been lived, their work finished, the cycle of their activity rounded off. One virtue of old age, then, is to live as fully at the height of one's powers as strength will permit, passing out of life serene and unreluctant, with willingness to live and yet with willingness to die. To know an old man who has grown old slowly, taking the seasons as they came, conserving the spirit of his youthful virtues, mellowing his philosophy of life, acquiring a clearer, saner, and more beautiful outlook on human nature and all its spiritual values with each passing year, is an education in the virtues of life. The virtues which produce an old age

97

such as this do not cut across the grain of life, but enhance and conserve the vital impulses and forces. Such an old age is the crowning evidence of the excellent working of the soul. A life needs no other proof than this that each season has known its proper virtue and healthful activity.

IV

THE LIFE OF IRONY

IV

THE LIFE OF IRONY

I COULD never, until recently, divest myself of the
haunting feeling that being ironical had something to do with the entering of the iron into one's
soul. I thought I knew what irony was, and I
admired it immensely. I could not believe that
there was something metallic and bitter about it.
Yet this sinister connotation of a clanging, rasp-
ing meanness of spirit, which I am sure it has
still in many people's minds, clung about it, until
one happy day my dictionary told me that the
iron had never entered into the soul at all, but the
soul into the iron (St. Jerome had read the psalm
wrong), and that irony was Greek, with all the
free, happy play of the Greek spirit about it, letting in fresh air and light into others' minds and
our own. It was to the Greek an incomparable
method of intercourse, the rub of mind against
mind by the simple use of simulated ignorance
and the adoption, without committing one's self,
of another's point of view. Not until I read the
Socrates of Plato did I fully appreciate that this

irony, — this pleasant challenging of the world,
this insistent judging of experience, this sense of
vivid contrasts and incongruities, of comic juxta-
positions, of flaring brilliancies, and no less heart-
breaking impossibilities, of all the little parts of
one's world being constantly set off against each
other, and made intelligible only by being trans-
lated into and defined in each others' terms, —
that this was a life, and a life of beauty, that one
might suddenly discover one's self living all un-
awares. And if one could judge one's own feeble
reflection, it was a life that had no room for iron
within its soul.

We should speak not of the Socratic method but
of the Socratic life. For irony is a life rather than
a method. A life cannot be taken off and put on
again at will; a method can. To be sure, some
people talk of life exactly as if it were some port-
able commodity, or some exchangeable garment.
We must live, they cry, as if we were about to
begin. And perhaps they are. Only some of us
would rather die than live that puny life that they
can adopt and cover themselves with. Irony is
too rich and precious a thing to be capable of such
transmission. The ironist is born and not made.
This critical attitude towards life, this delicious

sense of contrasts that we call irony, is not a pose or an amusement. It is something that colors every idea and every feeling of the man who is so happy as to be endowed with it.

Most people will tell you, I suppose, that the religious conviction of salvation is the only permanently satisfying coloring of life. In the splendid ironists, however, one sees a sweeter, more flexible and human principle of life, adequate, without the buttress of supernatural belief, to nourish and fortify the spirit. In the classic ironist of all time, irony shows an inherent nobility, a nobility that all ages have compared favorably with the Christian ideal. Lacking the spur of religious emotion, the sweetness of irony may be more difficult to maintain than the mood of belief. But may it not for that very reason be judged superior, for is it not written, He that endureth unto the end shall be saved?

It is not easy to explain the quality of that richest and most satisfying background of life. It lies, I think, in a vivid and intense feeling of aliveness which it gives. Experience comes to the ironist in little darts or spurts, with the added sense of contrast. Most men, I am afraid, see each bit of personal experience as a unit, strung more or less loosely on a string of other mildly related bits. But the man with the ironical temperament is forced constantly to compare and contrast his experience with what was, or what might be, or with what ought to be, and it is the shocks of these comparisons and contrasts that make up his inner life. He thinks he leads a richer life, because he feels not only the individual bits but the contrasts besides in all their various shadings and tints. To this sense of impingement of facts upon life is due a large part of this vividness of irony; and the rest is due to the alertness of the ironical mind. The ironist is always critically awake. He is always judging, and watching with inexhaustible interest, in order that he may judge. Now irony in its best sense is an exquisite sense of proportion, a sort of spiritual tact in judging the values and significances of experience. This sense of being spiritually alive which ceaseless criticism of the world we live in gives us, combined with the sense of power which free and untrammeled judging produces in us, is the background of irony. And it should be a means to the truest goodness.

Socrates made one mistake, — knowledge is not goodness. But it is a step towards judging, and good judgment is the true goodness. For it is on judgment impelled by desire that we act. The clearer and cleaner our judgments then, the more definite and correlated our actions. And the great value of these judgments of irony is that they are not artificial but spring naturally out of life. Irony, the science of comparative experience, compares things not with an established standard but with each other, and the values that slowly emerge from the process, values that emerge from one's own vivid reactions, are constantly revised, corrected, and refined by that same sense of contrast. The ironic life is a life keenly alert, keenly sensitive, reacting promptly with feelings of liking or dislike to each bit of experience, letting none of it pass without interpretation and assimilation, a life full and satisfying, — indeed a rival of the religious life.

The life of irony has the virtues of the religious life without its defects. It expresses the aggressive virtues without the quiescence of resignation. For the ironist has the courageous spirit, the sympathetic heart and the understanding mind, and can give them full play, unhampered by the searching introspection of the religious mind that often weakens rather than ennobles and fortifies. He is at one with the religious man in that he hates apathy and stagnation, for they mean death. But he is superior in that he attacks apathy of intellect and personality as well as apathy of emotion. He has a great conviction of the significance of all life, the lack of which conviction is the most saddening feature of the religious temperament. The religious man pretends that every aspect of life has meaning for him, but in practice he constantly minimizes the noisier and vivider elements. He is essentially an aristocrat in his interpretation of values, while the ironist is incorrigibly a democrat. Religion gives a man an intimacy with a few selected and rarified virtues and moods, while irony makes him a friend of the poor and lowly among spiritual things. When the religious man is healing and helping, it is at the expense of his spiritual comfort; he must tear himself away from his companions and go out grimly and sacrificingly into the struggle. The ironist, living his days among the humbler things, feels no such severe call to service. And yet the ironist, since he has no citadel of truth to defend, is really the more adventurous. Life, not fixed in predestined formulas or measurable by fixed, immutable standards, is fluid, rich and exciting. To the ironist it is both discovery and creation. His courage seeks out the obscure places of human personality, and his sympathy and understanding create new interests and enthusiasms in the other minds upon which they play. And these new interests in turn react upon his own life, discovering unexpected vistas there, and creating new insight into the world that he lives in. That democratic, sympathetic outlook upon the feelings and thoughts and actions of men and women is the life of irony.

That life is expressed in the social intercourse of ourselves with others. The daily fabric of the life of irony is woven out of our critical communings with ourselves and the personalities of our friend, and the people with whom we come in contact. The ironist, by adopting another's point of view and making it his own in order to carry light and air into it, literally puts himself in the other man's place. Irony is thus the truest sympathy. It is no cheap way of ridiculing an opponent by putting on his clothes and making fun of him. The ironist has no opponent, but only a friend. And in his irony he is helping that friend to reveal himself. That half-seriousness, that solemn treatment of the trivial and trivial treatment of the solemn which is the pattern of the ironist's talk is but his way of exhibiting the unexpected contrasts and shadings that he sees to be requisite to the keenest understanding of the situation. The ironist borrows and exchanges and appropriates ideas and gives them a new setting in juxtaposition with others, but he never burlesques or caricatures or exaggerates them. If an idea is absurd, the slightest change of environment will show that absurdity. The mere transference of an idea to another's mouth will bring to light all its hidden meaninglessness. It needs no extraneous aid. If an idea is hollow, it will show itself cowering against the intellectual background of the ironist like the puny, shivering thing it is. If a point of view cannot bear being adopted by another person, if it is not hardy enough to be transplanted, it has little right to exist at all. This world is no hothouse for ideas and attitudes. Too many outworn ideas are skulking in dark retreats, sequestered from the light; every man has great sunless stretches in his soul where base prejudices lurk and flourish. On these the white light of irony is needed to play. And it delights the ironist to watch them shrivel and decay under that light. The little tabooed regions of well-bred people, the " things we never mention," the basic biases and assumptions that underlie the lives and thinking of every class and profession, our second-hand dogmas and phrases, — all these live and thrive because they have never been transplanted, or heard from the lips of another. The dictum that "the only requisites for success are honesty and merit," which we applaud so frantically from the lips of the successful, becomes a ghastly irony in the mouth of an unemployed workingman. There would be a frightful mortality of points of view could we have a perfectly free exchange such as this. Irony is just this temporary borrowing and lending. Many of our cherished ideals would lose half their validity were they put bodily into the mouths of the less fortunate. But if irony destroys some ideals it builds up others. It tests ideals by their social validity, by their general interchangeability among all sorts of people and the world, but if it leaves the foundations of many in a shaky condition and renders more simply provisional, those that it does leave standing are imperishably founded in the common democratic experience of all men.

To the ironist it seems that the irony is not in the speaking but in the things themselves. He is a poor ironist who would consciously distort, or attempt to make another's idea appear in any light except its own. Absurdity is an intrinsic quality of so many things that they only have to be touched to reveal it. The deadliest way to annihilate the unoriginal and the insincere is to let it speak for itself. Irony is this letting things speak for themselves and hang themselves by their own rope. Only, it repeats the words after the speaker, and adjusts the rope. It is the commanding touch of a comprehending personality that dissolves the seemingly tough husk of the idea. The ironical method might be compared to the acid that develops a photographic plate. It does not distort the image, but merely brings clearly to the light all that was implicit in the plate before. And if it brings the picture to the light with values reversed, so does irony revel in a paradox, which is simply a photographic negative of the truth, truth with the values reversed. But turn the negative ever so slightly so that the light falls upon it, and the perfect picture appears in all its true values and beauty. Irony, we may say then, is the photography of the soul. The picture goes through certain changes in the hands of the ironist, but without these changes the truth would be simply a blank, unmeaning surface. The photograph is a synonym for deadly accuracy. Similarly the ironist insists always on seeing things as they are. He is a realist, whom the grim satisfaction of seeing the truth compensates for any sordidness that it may bring along with it. Things as they are, thrown against the background of things as they ought to be, — this is the ironist's vision. I should like to feel that the vision of the religious man is not too often things as they are, thrown against the background of things as they ought not to be.

The ironist is the only man who makes any serious attempt to distinguish between fresh and second-hand experience. Our minds are so unfortunately arranged that all sorts of beliefs can be accepted and propagated quite independently of any rational or even experimental basis at all. Nature does not seem to care very much whether our ideas are true or not, as long as we get on through life safely enough. And it is surprising on what an enormous amount of error we can get along comfortably. We cannot be wrong on every point or we should cease to live, but so long as we are empirically right in our habits, the truth or falsity of our ideas seems to have little effect upon our comfort. We are born into a world that is an inexhaustible store of ready-made ideas, stored up in tradition, in books, and in every medium of communication between our minds and others.

111

All we have to do is to accept this predigested nourishment, and ask no questions. We could live a whole life without ever making a really individual response, without providing ourselves out of our own experience with any of the material that our mind works on. Many of us seem to be just this kind of spiritual parasites. We may learn and absorb and grow, up to a certain point. But eventually something captures us: we become encased in a suit of armor, and invulnerable to our own experience. We have lost the faculty of being surprised. It is this encasing that the ironist fears, and it is the ironical method that he finds the best for preventing it. Irony keeps the waters in motion, so that the ice never has a .chance to form. The cut-and-dried life is easy to form because it has no sense of contrast; everything comes to one on its own terms, vouching for itself, and is accepted or rejected on its own good looks, and not for its fitness and place in the scheme of things.

This is the courage and this the sympathy of irony. Have they not a beauty of their own comparable in excellence with the paler glow of religious virtue? And the understanding of the ironist although aggressive and challenging has its justification, too. For he is mad to understand the world, to get to the bottom of other personalities. That is the reason for his constant classification. The ironist is the most dogmatic of persons. To understand you he must grasp you firmly, or he must pin you down definitely; if he accidentally nails you fast to a dogma that you indignantly repudiate, you must blame his enthusiasm and not his method. Dogmatism is rarely popular, and the ironist of course suffers. It hurts people's eyes to see a strong light, and the pleasant mist-land of ideas is much more emotionally warming than the clear, sunny region of transmissible phrases. How the average person wriggles and squirms under these piercing attempts to corner his personality! "Tell me what you mean!" or "What do you see in it?" are the fatal questions that the ironist puts, and who shall censure him if he does display the least trace of malicious delight as he watches the half-formed baby ideas struggle towards the light, or scurry around frantically to find some decent costume in which they may appear in public?

The judgments of the ironist are often discounted as being too sweeping. But he has a valid defense. Lack of classification is annihilation of thought. Even the newest philosophy will admit that classification is a necessary evil. Concepts are indispensable, — and yet each concept falsifies. The ironist must have as large a stock as possible, but he must have a stock. And even the unjust classification is marvelously effective. The ironist's name for his opponent is a challenge to him. The more sweeping it is, the more stimulus it gives him to repel the charge. He must explain just how he is unique and individual in his attitude. And in this explanation he reveals and discovers all that the ironist wishes to know about him. A handful of epithets is thus the ammunition of the ironist. He must call things by what seem to him to be their right names. In a sense, the ironist assumes the prisoner to be guilty until he proves himself innocent; but it is always in order that justice may be done, and that he may come to learn the prisoner's soul and all the wondrous things that are contained there.

It is this passion for comprehension that explains the ironist's apparently scandalous propensity to publicity. Nothing seems to him too sacred to touch, nothing too holy for him to become witty about. There are no doors locked to him, there is nothing that can make good any claim of resistance to scrutiny. His free and easy

114

manner of including everything within the sweep
of his vision is but his recognition, however, of
the fact that nothing is really so serious as we
think it is, and nothing quite so petty. The
ironist will descend in a moment from a discussion
of religion to a squabble over a card-game, and he
will defend himself with the reflection that religion is after all a human thing and must be discussed in the light of everyday living, and that
the card-game is an integral part of life, reveals
the personalities of the players — and his own to
himself — and being worthy of his interest is
worthy of his enthusiasm. The ironist is apt to
test things by their power to interest as much as
by their nobility, and if he sees the incongruous
and inflated in the lofty, so he sees the significant
in the trivial and raises it from its low degree.
Many a mighty impostor does he put down from
his seat. The ironist is the great intellectual democrat, in whose presence and before whose law all
ideas and attitudes stand equal. In his world
there is no privileged caste, no aristocracy of sentiments to be reverenced, or segregated systems of
interests to be tabooed. Nothing human is alien
to the ironist; the whole world is thrown open
naked to the play of his judgment.

In the eyes of its detractors, irony has all the vices of democracy. Its publicity seems mere vulgarity, its free hospitality seems to shock all ideas of moral worth. The ironist is but a scoffer, they say, with weapon leveled eternally at all that is good and true and sacred. The adoption of another's point of view seems little better than malicious dissimulation, — the repetition of others' words, an elaborate mockery; the ironist's eager interest seems a mere impudence or a lack of finer instincts; his interest in the trivial, the last confession of a mean spirit; and his love of classifying, a proof of his poverty of imaginative resource. Irony, in other words, is thought to be synonymous with cynicism. But the ironist is no cynic. His is a kindly, not a sour interest in human motives. He wants to find out how the human machine runs, not to prove that it is a worthless, broken-down affair. He accepts it as it comes, and if he finds it curiously feeble and futile in places, blame not him but the nature of things. He finds enough rich compensation in the unexpected charm that he constantly finds himself eliciting. The ironist sees life steadily and sees it whole; the cynic only a distorted fragment.

If the ironist is not cynic, neither is he merely a

dealer in satire, burlesque and ridicule. Irony
may be the raw material, innocent in itself but
capable of being put to evil uses. But it involves
neither the malice of satire, nor the horse-play
of burlesque, nor the stab of ridicule. Irony is infinitely finer and more delicate and impersonal.
The satirist is always personal and concrete, but
the ironist deals with general principles, and broad
aspects of human nature. It cannot be too much
emphasized that the function of the ironist is not
to make fun of people, but to give their souls an
airing. The ironist is a judge on the bench, giving
men a public hearing. He is not an aggressive
spirit who goes about seeking whom he may de-
vour, or a spiritual lawyer who courts litigation,
but the judge before whom file all the facts of his
experience, the people he meets, the opinions he
hears or reads, his own attitudes and prepposses-
sions. If any are convicted they are self-convicted.
The judge himself is passive, merciful, lenient.
There is judgment, but no punishment. Or rather,
the trial itself is the punishment. Now satire is all
that irony is not. The satirist is the aggressive
lawyer, fastening upon particular people and
particular qualities. But irony is no more personal than the sun that sends his flaming darts

into the world. The satirist is a purely practical man, with a business instinct, bent on the main chance and the definite object. He is often brutal, and always overbearing; the ironist never. Irony may wound from the very fineness and delicacy of its attack, but the wounding is incidental. The sole purpose of the satirist and the burlesquer is to wound, and they test their success by the deepness of the wound. But irony tests its own by the amount of generous light and air it has set flowing through an idea or a personality, and the broad significance it has revealed in neglected things.

If irony is not brutal, neither is it merely critical and destructive. The world has some reason, it is true, to complain against the rather supercilious judiciousness of the ironist. " Who are you to judge us?" it cries. The world does not like to feel the scrutinizing eyes of the ironist as he sits back in his chair; does not like to feel that the ironist is simply studying it and amusing himself at its expense. It is uneasy, and acts sometimes as if it did not have a perfectly clear conscience. To this uncomfortableness the ironist can retort, — "What is it that you are afraid to have known about you?" If the judgment amuses him, so much the worse for the world. But if the idea of

118

the ironist as judge implies that his attitude is wholly detached, wholly objective, it is an unfortunate metaphor. For he is as much part and parcel of the human show as any of the people he studies. The world is no stage, with the ironist as audience. His own personal reactions with the people about him form all the stuff of his thoughts and judgments. He has a personal interest in the case; his own personality is inextricably mingled in the stream of impressions that flows past him. If the ironist is destructive, it is his own world that he is destroying; if he is critical, it is his own world that he is criticizing. And his irony is his critique of life.

This is the defense of the ironist against the charge that he has a purely æsthetic attitude towards life. Too often, perhaps, the sparkling clarity of his thought, the play of his humor, the easy sense of superiority and intellectual command that he carries off, make his irony appear as rather the æsthetic nourishment of his life than an active way of doing and being. His rather detached air makes him seem to view people as means, not ends in themselves. With his delight in the vivid and poignant he is prone to see picturesqueness in the sordid, and tolerate evils that he should condemn.

119

For all his interest and activity, it is said that he does not really care. But this æsthetic taint to his irony is really only skin-deep. The ironist is ironical not because he does not care, but because he cares too much. He is feeling the profoundest depths of the world's great beating, laboring heart, and his playful attitude towards the grim and sordid is a necessary relief from the tension of too much caring. It is his salvation from unutterable despair. The terrible urgency of the reality of poverty and misery and exploitation would be too strong upon him. Only irony can give him a sense of proportion, and make his life fruitful and resolute. It can give him a temporary escape, a slight momentary reconciliation, a chance to draw a deep breath of resolve before plunging into the fight. It is not a palliative so much as a perspective. This is the only justification of the æsthetic attitude, that, if taken provisionally, it sweetens and fortifies. It is only deadly when adopted as absolute. The kind of æsthetic irony that Pater and Omar display is a paralyzed, half-seeing, half-caring reflection on life, — a tame, domesticated irony with its wings cut, an irony that furnishes a justification and a command to inaction. It is the result not of exquisitely refined feelings, but of social anæsthesia. Their irony, cut off from the great world of men and women and boys and girls and their intricate interweavings and jostlings and incongruities, turns pale and sickly and numb. The ironist has no right to see beauty in things unless he really cares. The æsthetic sense is harmless only when it is both ironical and social.

Irony is thus a cure for both optimism and pessimism. Nothing is so revolting to the ironist as the smiling optimist, who testifies in his fatuous heedlessness to the desirability of this best of all possible worlds. But the ironist has always an incorrigible propensity to see the other side. The hopeless maladjustment of too many people to their world, of their bondage in the iron fetters of circumstance, — all this is too glaring for the ironist's placidity. When he examines the beautiful picture, too often the best turns worst to him. But if optimism is impossible to the ironist, so is pessimism. The ironist may have a secret respect for the pessimist, — he at least has felt the bitter tang of life, and has really cared,— but he feels that the pessimist lacks. For if the optimist is blind, the pessimist is hypnotized. He is abnormally suggestive to evil. But clear-sighted irony sees that the world is too big and multifarious to be evil at heart. Something beautiful and joyous lurks even in the most hapless, — a child's laugh in a dreary street, a smile on the face of a weary woman. It is this saving quality of irony that both optimist and pessimist miss. And since plain common sense tells us that things are never quite so bad or quite so good as they seem, the ironist carries conviction into the hearts of men in their best moments.

The ironist is a person who counts in the world. He has all sorts of unexpected effects on both the people he goes with and himself. His is an insistent personality; he is as troublesome as a missionary. And he is a missionary; for, his own purpose being a comprehension of his fellows' souls, he makes them conscious of their own souls. He is a hard man; he will take nothing on reputation; he will guarantee for himself the qualities of things. He will not accept the vouchers of the world that a man is wise, or clever, or sincere, behind the impenetrable veil of his face. He must probe until he elicits the evidence of personality, until he gets at the peculiar quality which distinguishes that individual soul. For the ironist is after all a connoisseur in personality, and if his conversation partakes too often of the character of cross-examination, it is only as a lover of the beautiful, a possessor of taste, that he inquires. He does not want to see people squirm, but he does want to see whether they are alive or not. If he pricks too hard, it is not from malice, but merely from error in his estimation of the toughness of their skins. What people are inside is the most interesting question in the world to the ironist. And in finding out he stirs them up. Many a petty doubting spirit does he challenge and bully into a sort of self-respect. And many a bag of wind does he puncture. But his most useful function is this of stimulating thought and action. The ironist forces his friends to move their rusty limbs and unhinge the creaking doors of their minds. The world needs more ironists. Shut up with one's own thoughts, one loses the glow of life that comes from frank exchange of ideas with many kinds of people. Too many minds are stuffy, dusty rooms into which the windows have never been opened, — minds heavy with their own crotchets, cluttered up with untested theories and conflicting sympathies that have never got related in any social way. The ironist blows them all helterskelter, sweeps away the dust, and sets everything

in its proper place again. Your solid, self-respect-
ful mind, the ironist confesses he can do little
with; it is not of his world. He comes to freshen
and tone up the stale minds. The ironist is the
great purger and cleanser of life. Irony is a sort
of spiritual massage, rubbing the souls of men.
It may seem rough to some tender souls, but it
does not sere or scar them. The strong arm of the
ironist restores the circulation, and drives away
anæmia.

On the ironist himself the effect of irony is even
more invigorating. We can never really understand ourselves without at least a touch of irony.
The interpretation of human nature without is a
simple matter in comparison with the comprehension of that complex of elations and disgusts,
inhibitions and curious irrational impulses that we
call ourselves. It is not true that by examining
ourselves and coming to an understanding of the
way we behave we understand other people, but
that by the contrasts and little revelations of our
friends we learn to interpret ourselves. Introspection is no match for irony as a guide. The most
illuminating experience that we can have is a
sudden realization that had we been in the other
person's place we should have acted precisely as

hé did. To the ironist this is no mere intellectual conviction that, after all, none of us are perfect, but a vivid emotional experience which has knit him with that other person in one moment in a bond of sympathy that could have been acquired in no other way. Those minds that lack the touch of irony are too little flexible, or too heavily buttressed with self-esteem to make this sudden change of attitudes. The ironist, one might almost say, gets his brotherhood intuitively, feels the sympathy and the oneness in truth before he thinks them. The ironist is the only man who really gets outside of himself. What he does for other people, — that is, picking out a little piece of their souls and holding it up for their inspection, — he does for himself. He gets thus an objective view of himself. The unhealthy indoor brooding of introspection is artificial and unproductive, because it has no perspective or contrast. But the ironist with his constant outdoor look sees his own foibles and humiliations in the light of those of other people. He acquires a more tolerant, half-amused, half-earnest attitude toward himself. His self-respect is nourished by the knowledge that whatever things discreditable and foolish and worthless he has done, he has seen them approximated by others, and yet his esteem is kept safely pruned down by the recurring evidence that nothing he has is unique. He is poised in life, ready to soar or to walk as the occasion demands. He is pivoted, susceptible to every stimulus, and yet chained so that he cannot be flung off into space by his own centrifugal force.

Irony has the same sweetening and freshening effect on one's own life that it has on the lives of those who come in contact with it. It gives one a command of one's resources. The ironist practices a perfect economy of material. For he must utilize his wealth constantly and over and over again in various shapes and shadings. He may be poor in actual material, but out of the contrast and arrangement of that slender store he is able, like a kaleidoscope, to make a multifarious variety of wonderful patterns. His current coin is, so to speak, kept bright by constant exchange. He is infinitely richer than your opulent but miserly minds that hoard up facts, and are impotent from the very plethora of their accumulations.

Irony is essential to any real honesty. For dishonesty is at bottom simply an attempt to save somebody's face. But the ironist does not want any faces saved, neither his own nor those of other people. To save faces is to sophisticate human nature, to falsify the facts, and miss a delicious contrast, an illuminating revelation of how people act. So the ironist is the only perfectly honest man. But he suffers for it by acquiring a reputation for impudence. His willingness to bear the consequences of his own acts, his quiet insistence that others shall bear consequences, seem like mere shamelessness, a lack of delicate feeling for "situations." But accustomed as he is to range freely and know no fear nor favor, he despises this reserve as a species of timidity or even hypocrisy. It is an irony itself that the one temperament that can be said really to appreciate human nature, in the sense of understanding it rightly, should be called impudent, and it is another that it should be denounced as monstrously egotistical. The ironical mind is the only truly modest mind, for its point of view is ever outside itself. If it calls attention to itself, it is only as another of those fascinating human creatures that pass ever by with their bewildering, alluring ways. If it talks about itself, it is only as a third person in whom all the talkers are supposed to be eagerly interested. In this sense the ironist has lost his egotism completely. He has rubbed out the line that separates his personality from the rest of the world.

The ironist must take people very seriously, to spend so much time over them. He must be both serious and sincere or he would not persist in his irony and expose himself to so much misunderstanding. And since it is not how people treat him, but simply how they act, that furnishes the basis for his appreciation, the ironist finds it easy to forgive. He has a way of letting the individual offense slide, in favor of a deeper principle. In the act of being grossly misrepresented, he can feel a pang of exasperated delight that people should be so dense; in the act of being taken in, he can feel the cleverness of it all. He becomes for the moment his enemy; and we can always forgive ourselves. Even while he is being insulted, or outraged or ignored, he can feel, "After all, this is what life is! This is the way we poor human creatures behave!" The ironist is thus in a sense vicarious human nature. Through that deep, anticipatory sympathy, he is kept clean from hate or scorn.

The ironist therefore has a valid defense against all the charges of brutality and triviality and irreverence, that the religious man is prone to bring against him. He can care more deeply about things because he can see so much more widely. And he can take life very seriously because it interests him so intensely. And he can feel its poignancy and its flux more keenly because he delivers himself up bravely to its swirling, many-hued current. The inner peace of religion seems gained only at the expense of the reality of living. A life such as the life of irony, lived fully and joyously, cannot be peaceful; it cannot even be happy, in the sense of calm content and satisfaction. But it can be better than either — it can be wise, and it can be fruitful. And it can be good, in a way that the life of inner peace cannot be. For the life of irony having no reserve and weaving itself out of the flux of experience rather than out of eternal values has the broad, honest sympathy of democracy, that is impossible to any temperament with the aristocratic taint. One advantage the religious life has is a salvation in another world to which it can withdraw. The life of irony has laid up few treasures in heaven, but many in this world. Having gained so much it has much to lose. But its glory is that it can lose nothing unless it lose all.

To shafts of fortune and blows of friends or

enemies then, the ironist is almost impregnable. He knows how to parry each thrust and prepare for every emergency. Even if the arrows reach him, all the poison has been sucked out of them by his clear, resolute understanding of their significance. There is but one weak spot in his armor, but one disaster that he fears more almost than the loss of his life, — a shrinkage of his environment, a running dry of experience. He fears to be cut off from friends and crowds and human faces and speech and books, for he demands to be ceaselessly fed. Like a modern city, he is totally dependent on a steady flow of supplies from the outside world, and will be in danger of starvation, if the lines of communication are interrupted. Without people and opinions for his mind to play on, his irony withers and faints. He has not the faculty of brooding; he cannot mine the depths of his own soul, and bring forth after labor mighty nuggets of thought. The flow and swirl of things is his compelling interest. His thoughts are reactions, immediate and vivid, to his daily experience. Some deep, unconscious brooding must go on, to produce that happy precision of judgment of his; but it is not voluntary. He is conscious only of the shifting light and play of life; his

130

world is dynamic, energetic, changing. He lives in a world of relations, and he must have a whole store of things to be related. He has lost himself completely in this world he lives in. His ironical interpretation of the world is his life, and this world is his nourishment. Take away this environmental world and you have slain his soul. He is invulnerable to everything except that deprivation.

V

THE EXCITEMENT OF FRIENDSHIP

V

THE EXCITEMENT OF FRIENDSHIP

My friends, I can say with truth, since I have no other treasure, are my fortune. I really live only when I am with my friends. Those sufficient persons who can pass happily long periods of solitude communing with their own thoughts and nourishing their own souls fill me with a despairing admiration. Their gift of auto-stimulation argues a personal power which I shall never possess. Or else it argues, as I like to think in self-defense, a callousness of spirit, an insensitiveness to the outside influences which nourish and sustain the more susceptible mind. And those persons who can shut themselves up for long periods and work out their thoughts alone, constructing beautiful and orderly representations of their own spirits, are to me a continual mystery. I know this is the way that things are accomplished, that "monotony and solitude" are necessary for him who would produce creative thought. Yet, knowing well this truth, I shun them both. I am a battery that needs to be often recharged. I require the excitement of friendship; I must have the constant stimulation of friends. I do not spark automatically, but must have other minds to rub up against, and strike from them by friction the spark that will kindle my thoughts.

When I walk, I must have a friend to talk to, or I shall not even think. I am not of those who, like Stevenson, believe that walking should be a kind of vegetative stupor, where the sun and air merely fill one with a diffused sense of well-being and exclude definite thought. The wind should rather blow through the dusty regions of the mind, and the sun light up its dark corners, and thinking and talking should be saner and higher and more joyful than within doors. But one must have a friend along to open the windows. Neither can I sympathize with those persons who carry on long chains of reasoning while they are traveling or walking. When alone, my thinking is as desultory as the scenery of the roadside, and when with a friend, it is apt to be as full of romantic surprises as a walk through a woodland glen. Good talk is like good scenery — continuous yet constantly varying, and full of the charm of novelty and surprise. How unnatural it is to think except when one is forced to do it, is discovered when one attempts to analyze one's thoughts when alone. He is a rare genius who finds something beyond the mere visual images that float through his mind, — either the reflection of what he is actually seeing, or the pictorial representations of what he has been doing or what he wants or intends to do in the near or far future. We should be shocked to confess to ourselves how little control we have over our own minds; we shall be lucky if we can believe that we guide them.

Thinking, then, was given us for use in emergencies, and no man can be justly blamed if he reserves it for emergencies. He can be blamed, however, if he does not expose himself to those crises which will call it forth. Now a friend is such an emergency, perhaps the most exciting stimulus to thinking that one can find, and if one wants to live beyond the vegetative stupor, one must surround one's self with friends. I shall call my friends, then, all those influences which warm me and start running again all my currents of thought and imagination. The persons, causes, and books that unlock the prison of my intellectual torpor, I can justly call my friends, for I find that I feel toward them all the same eager joy and inexhaustible rush of welcome. Where they differ it shall be in degree and not in kind. The speaker whom I hear, the book that I read, the friend with whom I chat, the music that I play, even the blank paper before me, which subtly stirs me to cover it with sentences that unfold surprisingly and entice me to follow until I seem hopelessly lost from the trail, — all these shall be my friends as long as I find myself responding to them, and no longer. They are all alike in being emergencies that call upon me for instant and definite response.

The difference between them lies in their response to me. My personal friends react upon me; the lecturers and books and music and pictures do not. These are not influenced by my feelings or by what I do. I can approach them cautiously or boldly, respond to them slowly or warmly, and they will not care. They have a definite quality, and do not change; if I respond differently to them at different times, I know that it is I and not they who have altered. The excitement of friendship does not lie with them. One feels this lack particularly in reading, which no amount of enthusiasm can make more than a feeble and spiritless performance. The more enthusiasm the reading inspires in one, the more one rebels at the passivity into which one is forced. I want to get somehow at grips with the book. I can feel the warmth of the personality behind it, but I cannot see the face as I can the face of a person, lighting and changing with the iridescent play of expression. It is better with music; one can get at grips with one's piano, and feel the resistance and the response of the music one plays. One gets the sense of aiding somehow in its creation, the lack of which feeling is the fatal weakness of reading, though itself the easiest and most universal of friendly stimulations. One comes from much reading with a sense of depression and a vague feeling of something unsatisfied; from friends or music one comes with a high sense of elation and of the brimming adequacy of life.

If one could only retain those moments! What a tragedy it is that our periods of stimulated thinking should be so difficult of reproduction; that there is no intellectual shorthand to take down the keen thoughts, the trains of argument, the pregnant thoughts, which spring so spontaneously to the mind at such times! What a tragedy that one must wait till the fire has died out, till the light has faded away, to transcribe the dull flickering remembrances of those golden hours when thought and feeling seemed to have melted together, and one said and thought what seemed truest and finest and most worthy of one's immortalizing! This is what constitutes the hopeless labor of writing, — that one must struggle constantly to warm again the thoughts that are cold or have been utterly consumed. What was thought in the hours of stimulation must be written in the hours of solitude, when the mind is apt to be cold and gray, and when one is fortunate to find on the hearth of the memory even a few scattered embers lying about. The blood runs sluggish as one sits down to write. What worry and striving it takes to get it running freely again! What labor to reproduce even a semblance of what seemed to come so genially and naturally in the contact and intercourse of friendship!

One of the curious superstitions of friendship is that we somehow choose our friends. To the connoisseur in friendship no idea could be more amazing and incredible. Our friends are chosen for us by some hidden law of sympathy, and not by our conscious wills. All we know is that in our reactions to people we are attracted to some and are indifferent to others. And the ground of this mutual interest seems based on no discoverable principles of similarity of temperament or character. We have no time, when meeting a new person, to study him or her carefully; our reactions are swift and immediate. Our minds are made up instantly, — "friend or non-friend." By some subtle intuitions, we know and have measured at their first words all the possibilities which their friendship has in store for us. We get the full quality of their personality at the first shock of meeting, and no future intimacy changes that quality.

If I am to like a man, I like him at once; further acquaintance can only broaden and deepen that liking and understanding. If I am destined to respond, I respond at once or never. If I do not respond, he continues to be to me as if I had never met him; he does not exist in my world. His thoughts, feelings, and interests I can but dimly conceive of; if I do think of him it is only as a member of some general class. My imaginative sympathy can embrace him only as a type. If his interests are in some way forced upon my attention, and my imagination is compelled to encompass him as an individual, I find his ideas and interests appearing like pale, shadowy things, dim ghosts of the real world that my friends and I live in.

Association with such aliens — and how much of our life is necessarily spent in their company — is a torture far worse than being actually disliked. Probably they do not dislike us, but there is this strange gulf which cuts us off from their possible sympathy. A pall seems to hang over our spirits; our souls are dumb. It is a struggle and an effort to affect them at all. And though we may know that this depressing weight which seems to press on us in our intercourse with them has no existence, yet this realization does not cure our helplessness. We do not exist for them any more than they exist for us. They are depressants, not stimulators as are our friends. Our words sound singularly futile and half-hearted as they pass our lips. Our thoughts turn to ashes as we utter them. In the grip of this predestined antipathy we can do nothing but submit and pass on.

But in how different a light do we see our friends! They are no types, but each a unique, exhaustless personality, with his own absorbing little cosmos of interests round him. And those interests are real and vital, and in some way interwoven with one's own cosmos. Our friends are those whose worlds overlap our own, like intersecting circles. If there is too much overlapping,

142

however, there is monotony and a mutual cancellation. It is, perhaps, a question of attitude as much as anything. Our friends must be pointed in the same direction in which we are going, and the truest friendship and delight is when we can watch each other's attitude toward life grow increasingly similar; or if not similar, at least so sympathetic as to be mutually complementary and sustaining.

The wholesale expatriation from our world of all who do not overlap us or look at life in a similar direction is so fatal to success that we cannot afford to let these subtle forces of friendship and apathy have full sway with our souls. To be at the mercy of whatever preordained relations may have been set up between us and the people we meet is to make us incapable of negotiating business in a world where one must be all things to all men. From an early age, therefore, we work, instinctively or consciously, to get our reactions under control, so as to direct them in the way most profitable to us. By a slow and imperceptible accretion of impersonality over the erratic tendencies of personal response and feeling, we acquire the professional manner, which opens the world wide to us. We become human patterns of

143

the profession into which we have fallen, and are no longer individual personalities. Men find no difficulty in becoming soon so professionalized that their manner to their children at home is almost identical with that to their clients in the office. Such an extinction of the personality is a costly price to pay for worldly success. One has integrated one's character, perhaps, but at the cost of the zest and verve and peril of true friendship.

To those of us, then, who have not been tempted by success, or who have been so fortunate as to escape it, friendship is a life-long adventure. We do not integrate ourselves, and we have as many sides to our character as we have friends to show them to. Quite unconsciously I find myself witty with one friend, large and magnanimous with another, petulant and stingy with another, wise and grave with another, and utterly frivolous with another. I watch with surprise the sudden and startling changes in myself as I pass from the influence of one friend to the influence of some one else. But my character with each particular friend is constant. I find myself, whenever I meet him, with much the same emotional and mental tone. If we talk, there is with each one some definite subject upon which we always speak and which remains perennially fresh and new. If I am so unfortunate as to stray accidentally from one of these well-worn fields into another, I am instantly reminded of the fact by the strangeness and chill of the atmosphere. We are happy only on our familiar levels, but on these we feel that we could go on exhaustless forever, without a pang of ennui. And this inexhaustibility of talk is the truest evidence of good friendship.

Friends do not, on the other hand, always talk of what is nearest to them. Friendship requires that there be an open channel between friends, but it does not demand that that channel be the deepest in our nature. It may be of the shallowest kind and yet the friendship be of the truest. For all the different traits of our nature must get their airing through friends, the trivial as well as the significant. We let ourselves out piecemeal, it seems, so that only with a host of varied friends can we express ourselves to the fullest. Each friend calls out some particular trait in us, and it requires the whole chorus fitly to teach us what we are. This is the imperative need of friendship. A man with few friends is only half-developed; there are whole sides of his nature which are locked up and have never been expressed. He cannot unlock them himself, he cannot even discover them; friends alone can stimulate him and open them. Such a man is in prison; his soul is in penal solitude. A man must get friends as he would get food and drink for nourishment and sustenance. And he must keep them, as he would keep health and wealth, as the infallible safeguards against misery and poverty of spirit.

If it seems selfish to insist so urgently upon one's need for friends, if it should be asked what we are giving our friends in return for all their spiritual fortification and nourishment, the defense would have to be, that we give back to them in ample measure what they give to us. If we are their friends, we are stimulating them as they are stimulating us. They will find that they talk with unusual brilliancy when they are with us. And we may find that we have, perhaps, merely listened to them. Yet through that curious bond of sympathy which has made us friends, we have done as much for them as if we had exerted ourselves in the most active way. The only duty of friendship is that we and our friends should live at our highest and best when together. Having achieved that, we have fulfilled the law.

THE EXCITEMENT OF FRIENDSHIP

A good friendship, strange to say, has little place for mutual consolations and ministrations. Friendship breathes a more rugged air. In sorrow the silent pressure of the hand speaks the emotions, and lesser griefs and misfortunes are ignored or glossed over. The fatal facility of women's friendships, their copious outpourings of grief to each other, their sharing of wounds and sufferings, their half-pleased interest in misfortune, — all this seems of a lesser order than the robust friendships of men, who console each other in a much more subtle, even intuitive way, — by a constant pervading sympathy which is felt rather than expressed. For the true atmosphere of friendship is a sunny one. Griefs and disappointments do not thrive in its clear, healthy light. When they do appear, they take on a new color. The silver lining appears, and we see even our own personal mistakes and chagrins as whimsical adventures. It is almost impossible seriously to believe in one's bad luck or failures or incapacity while one is talking with a friend. One achieves a sort of transfiguration of personality in those moments. In the midst of the high and genial flow of intimate talk, a pang may seize one at the thought of the next day's drudgery, when life will be lived alone again; but nothing can dispel the ease and fullness with which it is being lived at the moment. It is, indeed, a heavy care that will not dissolve into misty air at the magic touch of a friend's voice.

Fine as friendship is, there is nothing irrevocable about it. The bonds of friendship are not iron bonds, proof against the strongest of strains and the heaviest of assaults. A man by becoming your friend has not committed himself to all the demands which you may be pleased to make upon him. Foolish people like to test the bonds of their friendships, pulling upon them to see how much strain they will stand. When they snap, it is as if friendship itself had been proved unworthy. But the truth is that good friendships are fragile things and require as much care in handling as any other fragile and precious things. For friendship is an adventure and a romance, and in adventures it is the unexpected that happens. It is the zest of peril that makes the excitement of friendship. All that is unpleasant and unfavorable is foreign to its atmosphere; there is no place in friendship for harsh criticism or fault-finding. We will "take less" from a friend than we will from one who is indifferent to us.

THE EXCITEMENT OF FRIENDSHIP

Good friendship is lived on a warm, impetuous plane; the long-suffering kind of friendship is a feeble and, at best, a half-hearted affair. It is friendship in the valley and not on the breezy heights. For the secret of friendship is a mutual admiration, and it is the realization or suspicion that that admiration is lessening on one side or the other that swiftly breaks the charm. Now this admiration must have in it no taint of adulation, which will wreck a friendship as soon as suspicion will. But it must consist of the conviction, subtly expressed in every tone of the voice, that each has found in the other friend a rare spirit, compounded of light and intelligence and charm. And there must be no open expression of this feeling, but only the silent flattery, soft and almost imperceptible.

And in the best of friendships this feeling is equal on both sides. Too great a superiority in our friend disturbs the balance, and casts a sort of artificial light on the talk and intercourse. We want to believe that we are fairly equal to our friends in power and capacity, and that if they excel us in one trait, we have some counterbalancing quality in another direction. It is the reverse side of this shield that gives point to the diabolical insight of the Frenchman who remarked that we were never heartbroken by the misfortunes of our best friends. If we have had misfortunes, it is not wholly unjust and unfortunate that our friends should suffer too. Only their misfortunes must not be worse than ours. For the equilibrium is then destroyed, and our serious alarm and sympathy aroused. Similarly we rejoice in the good fortune of our friends, always provided that it be not too dazzling or too undeserved.

It is these aspects of friendship, which cannot be sneered away by the reproach of jealousy, that make friendship a precarious and adventurous thing. But it is precious in proportion to its precariousness, and its littlenesses are but the symptoms of how much friends care, and how sensitive they are to all the secret bonds and influences that unite them.

Since our friends have all become woven into our very selves, to part from friends is to lose, in a measure, one's self. He is a brave and hardy soul who can retain his personality after his friends are gone. And since each friend is the key which unlocks an aspect of one's own personality, to lose a friend is to cut away a part of one's self. I may make another friend to replace the loss, but the

150

unique quality of the first friend can never be brought back. He leaves a wound which heals only gradually. To have him go away is as bad as to have him pass to another world. The letter is so miserable a travesty on the personal presence, a thin ghost of the thought of the once-present friend. It is as satisfactory as a whiff of stale tobacco smoke to the lover of smoking.

Those persons and things, then, that inspire us to do our best, that make us live at our best, when we are in their presence, that call forth from us our latent and unsuspected personality, that nourish and support that personality, — those are our friends. The reflection of their glow makes bright the darker and quieter hours when they are not with us. They are a true part of our widest self; we should hardly have a self without them. Their world is one where chagrin and failure do not enter. Like the sun-dial, they "only mark the shining hours."

VI

THE ADVENTURE OF LIFE

VI

THE ADVENTURE OF LIFE

THAT life is an adventure it needs nothing more
than the wonder of our being in the world and
the precariousness of our stay in it to inform us.
Although we are, perhaps, as the scientists tell
us, mere inert accompaniments of certain bundles
of organized matter, we tend incorrigibly to think
of ourselves as unique personalities. And as we let
our imagination roam over the world and dwell
on the infinite variety of scenes and thoughts and
feelings and forms of life, we wonder at the incredible marvel that has placed us just here in
this age and country and locality where we were
born. That it should be this particular place and
time and body that my consciousness is illuminating gives, indeed, the thrill of wonder and adventure to the mere fact of my becoming and
being.

And as life goes on, the feeling for the precariousness of that being grows upon one's mind. The
security of childhood gives place to an awareness

155

of the perils of misfortune, disease, and sudden death which seem to lie in wait for men and seize them without regard to their choices or deserts. We are prone, of course, to believe in our personal luck; it is the helplessness of others around us rather that impresses us, as we see both friends and strangers visited with the most dreadful evils, and with an impartiality of treatment that gradually tends to force upon us the conviction that we, too, are not immune. At some stage in our life, oftenest perhaps when the first flush of youth is past, we are suddenly thrown into a suspicion of life, a dread of nameless and unforeseeable ill, and a sober realization of the need of circumspection and defense. We discover that we live in a world where almost anything is likely to happen. Shocking accidents that cut men off in their prime, pain and suffering falling upon the just and the unjust, maladjustments and misunderstandings that poison and ruin lives, — all these things are daily occurrences in our experience, either of personal knowledge or out of that wider experience of our reading.

Religion seems to give little consolation in the face of such incontrovertible facts. For no belief in Providence can gainsay the seeming fact that

156

we are living in a world that is run without regard to the health and prosperity of its inhabitants. Whatever its ulterior meanings, they do not seem to be adjusted to our scale of values. Physical law we can see, but where are the workings of a moral law? If they are present, they seem to cut woefully against the grain of the best desires and feelings of men. Evil seems to be out of all proportion to the ability of its sufferers to bear it, or of its chastening and corrective efficacy. Our feelings are too sensitive for the assaults which the world makes upon them. If the responsibility for making all things work together for his good is laid entirely upon man, it is a burden too heavy for his weakness and ignorance to bear. And thus we contemplate the old, old problem of evil. And in its contemplation, the adventure of life, which should be a tonic and a spur, becomes a depressant; instead of nerving, it intimidates, and makes us walk cautiously and sadly through life, where we should ride fast and shout for joy.

In these modern days, the very wealth of our experience overwhelms us, and makes life harder to live in the sight of evil. The broadening of communication, giving us a connection through newspapers and magazines with the whole world, has made our experience almost as wide as the world. In that experience, however, we get all the world's horrors as well as its interests and delights. Thus has it been that this widening, which has meant the possibility of living the contemplative and imaginative life on an infinitely higher plane than before, has meant also a soul-sickness to the more sensitive, because of the immense and overburdening drafts on their sympathy which the new experience involved. Although our increased knowledge of the world has meant everywhere reform, and has vastly improved and beautified life for millions of men, it has at the same time opened a nerve the pain of which no opiate has been able to soothe. And along with the real increase of longevity and sounder health for civilized man, attained through the triumphs of medical science, there has come a renewed realization of the shortness and precariousness, at its best, of life. The fact that our knowledge of evil is shared by millions of men intensifies, I think, our sensitiveness. Through the genius of display writers, thousands of readers are enabled to be present imaginatively at scenes of horror. The subtle sense of a vast concourse having witnessed the scene magnifies its potency to the individual mind, and gives it the morbid touch as of crowds witnessing an execution.

Our forefathers were more fortunate, and could contemplate evil more philosophically and objectively. Their experience was happily limited to what the normal soul could endure. Their evil was confined to their vicinity. What dim intelligence of foreign disaster and misery leaked in, only served to purify and sober their spirits. Evil did not then reverberate around the world as it does now. Their nerves were not strained or made raw by the reiterations and expatiations on faraway pestilence and famine, gigantic sea disasters, wanton murders, or even the shocking living conditions of the great city slums. Their imaginations had opportunity to grow healthily, unassailed by the morbidities of distant evil, which seems magnified and ominous through its very strangeness. They were not forced constantly to ask themselves the question, "What kind of a world do we live in anyhow? Has it no mercy and no hope?" They were not having constantly thrown up to them a justification of the universe. Perhaps it was because they were more concerned with personal sin than with objective evil. The enormity of sin against their Maker blotted out all transient misfortune and death. But it was more likely that the actual ignorance of that evil permitted their personal flagrancies to loom up larger in their sight. Whatever the cause, there was a difference. We have only to compare their literature — solid, complacent, rational — with our restless and hectic stuff; or contrast their portraits — well-nourished, self-respecting faces — with the cheap or callous or hunted faces that we see about us to-day, to get the change in spiritual fibre which this opening of the world has wrought. It has been a real eating of the tree of the knowledge of good and evil. A social conscience has been born. An expansion of soul has been forced upon us. We have the double need of a broader vision to assimilate the good that is revealed to us, and a stronger courage to bear the evil with which our slowly-bettering old world still seems to reek.

But the youth of this modern generation are coming more and more to see that the gloom and hysteria of this restless age, with all the other seemingly neurotic symptoms of decay, are simply growing-pains. They signify a better spiritual health that is to be. The soul is now learning to adjust itself to the new conditions, to embrace

the wide world that is its heritage, and not to reel
and stagger before the assaults of a malign power.
Life will always be fraught with real peril, but it
is peril which gives us the sense of adventure.
And as we gain in our command over the resources, both material and spiritual, of the world,
we shall see the adventure as not so much the
peril of evil as an opportunity of permanent
achievement. We can only cure our suffering
from the evil in the world by doing all in our
power to wipe out that which is caused by human
blundering, and prevent what we can prevent by
our control of the forces of nature. Our own little
personal evils we can dismiss with little thought.
Such as have come to us we can endure, — for
have we not already endured them? — and those
that we dread we shall not keep away by fear or
worry. We can easily become as much slaves to
precaution as we can to fear. Although we can
never rivet our fortune so tight as to make it impregnable, we may by our excessive prudence
squeeze out of the life that we are guarding so
anxiously all the adventurous quality that makes
it worth living. In the light of our own problem-
atical misfortune, we must rather live freely and
easily, taking the ordinary chances and looking

To-morrow confidently in the face as we have looked To-day. I have come thus far safely and well; why may I not come farther?

But in regard to the evil that we see around us, the problem is more difficult. Though the youth of this generation hope to conquer, the battle is still on. We have fought our way to a knowledge of things as they are, and we must now fight our way beyond it. That first fight was our first sense of the adventure of life. Our purpose early became to track the world relentlessly down to its lair. We were resolute to find out the facts, no matter how sinister and barren they proved themselves to be. We would make no compromises with our desires, or with those weak persons who could not endure the clear light of reality. We were scornful in the presence of the superstitions of our elders. We could not conceive that sufficient knowledge combined with action would not be able to solve all our problems and make clear all our path. As our knowledge grew, so did our courage. We pressed more eagerly on the trail of this world of ours, purposing to capture and tame its mysteries, and reveal it as it is, so that none could doubt us. As we penetrated farther, however, into the cave, the path became

162

more and more uncertain. We discovered our
prey to be far grimmer and more dangerous than
we had ever imagined. As he turned slowly at
bay, we discovered that he was not only repuls-
ive but threatening. We were sternly prepared
to accept him just as we found him, exulting that
we should know things as they really were. We
were ready for the worst, and yet somehow not
for this worst. We had not imagined him retal-
iating upon us. In our first recoil, the thought
flashed upon us that our tracking him to his lair
might end in his feasting on our bones.

It is somewhat thus that we feel when the full
implications of the materialism to which we have
laboriously fought our way dawn upon us, or we
realize the full weight of the sodden social misery
around us. Hitherto we have been so intent on the
trail that we have not stopped to consider what
it all meant. Now that we know, not only our
own salvation seems threatened, but that of all
around us, even the integrity of the world itself.
In these moments of perplexity and alarm, we lose
confidence in ourselves and all our values and interpretations. To go further seems to be to court
despair. We are ashamed to retreat, and, besides,
have come too far ever to get back into the safe

plain of ignorance again. The world seems to be revealed to us as mechanical in its workings and fortuitous in its origin, and the warmth and light of beauty and ideals that we have known all along to be our true life seem to be proven illusions. And the wailing of the world comes up to us, cast off from any divine assistance, left to the mercy of its own weak wills and puny strengths. In this fall, our world itself seems to have lost merit, and we feel ourselves almost degraded by being a part of it. We have suddenly been deprived of our souls; the world seems to have beaten us in our first real battle with it.

Now this despair is partly the result of an excessive responsibility that we have taken for the universe. In youth, if we are earnest and eager, we tend to take every bit of experience that comes to us, as either a justification or a condemnation of the world. We are all instinctive monists at that age, and crave a complete whole. As we unconsciously construct our philosophy of life, each fact gets automatically recorded as confirming or denying the competency of the world we live in. Even the first shock of disillusionment, which banishes those dreams of a beautiful, orderly, and rational world that had suffused childhood with their golden light, did not shatter the conviction that there was somehow at least a Lord's side. The sudden closing of the account in the second shock, when the world turns on us, shows us how mighty has been the issue at stake, — nothing less than our faith in the universe, and, perhaps, in the last resort, of our faith in ourselves. We see now that our breathless seriousness of youth was all along simply a studying of our crowded experience to see whether it was on the Lord's side or not. And now in our doubt we are left with a weight on our souls which is not our own, a burden which we have really usurped.

In its adventure with evil, youth must not allow this strange, metaphysical responsibility to depress and incapacitate it. We shall never face life freely and bravely and worthily if we do. I may wonder, it is true, as I look out on these peaceful fields, with the warm sun and blue sky above me and the kindly faces of my good friends around me, how this can be the same world that houses the millions of poor and wretched people in their burning and huddled quarters in the city. Can these days, in which I am free to come and go and walk and study as I will, be the same that measure out the long hours of drudgery to thousands of youth amid the whir of machines, and these long restful nights of mine, the same that are for them only gasps breaking a long monotony? It must be the same world, however, whether we can ever reconcile ourselves to it or not. But we need plainly feel no responsibility for what happened previously to our generation. Our responsibility now is a collective, a social responsibility. And it is only for the evil that society might prevent were it organized wisely and justly. Beyond that it does not go. For the accidental evil that is showered upon the world, we are not responsible, and we need not feel either that the integrity of the universe is necessarily compromised by it. It is necessary to be somewhat self-centred in considering it. We must trust our own feelings rather than any rational proof. In spite of everything, the world seems to us so unconquerably good, it affords so many satisfactions, and is so rich in beauty and kindliness, that we have a right to assume that there is a side of things that we miss in our pessimistic contemplation of misfortune and disaster. We see only the outer rind of it. People usually seem to be so much happier than we can find any very rational excuse for their being, and that old world that confronted us and scared us may look very much worse than it really is. And we can remember that adding to the number of the sufferers does not intensify the actual quality of the suffering. There is no more suffering than one person can bear.

These considerations may allay a little our first terror and despair. When we really understand that the world is not damned by the evil in it, we shall be ready to see it in its true light as a challenge to our heroisms. Not how evil came into the world, but how we are going to get it out, becomes the problem. Not by brooding over the hopeless, but by laying plans for the possible will we shoulder our true responsibility. We shall find then that we had no need of despair. We were on the right track. When the world that we were tracking down turned at bay, he threatened more than he was able to perform. Not less science but more science do we need in order that we may more and more get into our control the forces and properties of nature, and guide them for our benefit. But we must learn that the interpretation of the world lies not in its mechanism but in its meanings, and those meanings we find in our values and ideals, which are very real to us. Science brings us only to an "area of our dwelling," as Whitman says. The moral adventure of the rising generation will be to learn this truth thoroughly, and to reinstate ideals and personality at the heart of the world.

Our most favorable battle-ground against evil will for some time at least be the social movement. Poverty and sin and social injustice we must feel not sentimentally nor so much a symptom of a guilty conscience as a call to coöperate with the exploited and sufferers in throwing off their ills. Sensitiveness to evil will be most fruitful when it rouses a youth to the practical encouragement of the under-men to save themselves. Youth to-day needs to "beat the gong of revolt." The oppressed seldom ask for our sympathy, and this is right and fitting; for they do not need it. (It might even make them contented with their lot.) What they need is the inspiration and the knowledge to come into their own. All we can ever do in the way of good to people is to encourage them to do good to themselves. "Who would be free, himself must strike the blow!" This is the social responsibility of modern youth. It must not seek to serve humanity so much as to rouse and teach it. The great moral adventure that lies still ahead of us is to call men to the expansion of their souls

to the wide world which has suddenly been revealed to them.

Perhaps with that expansion youth will finally
effect a reconciliation with life of those two supremest and most poignant of adventures: the
thoughts that cluster around sex, and the fears and
hopes that cluster around death, the one the gate-
way into life, the other out of it. Youth finds them
the two hardest aspects of life to adjust with the
rest of the world in which we live. They are ever-
present and pervasive, and yet their manifestations always cause us surprise, and shock us
as of something unwonted intruding in our daily
affairs. They are the unseen spectres behind life,
of which we are always dimly conscious, but
which we are always afraid to meet boldly and
face to face. We speak of them furtively, or in
far-away poetical strains. They are the materials
for the tragedies of life, of its pathos and wistfulness, of its splendors and defeats. Yet they are
treated always with an incorrigible and dishonest
delicacy. The world, youth soon finds, is a much
less orderly and refined place than would appear
on the surface of our daily intercourse and words.
As we put on our best clothes to appear in public,

so the world puts on its best clothes to appear in talk and print.

Men ignore death, as if they were quite unconscious that it would sometime come to them, yet who knows how many pensive or terrible moments the thought gives them? But the spectre is quite invisible to us. Or if they have passions, and respond as sensitively as a vibrating string to sex influences and appeals, we have little indication of that throbbing life behind the impenetrable veil of their countenances. We can know what people think about all other things, even what they think about God, but what they think of these two adventures of sex and death we never know. It is not so much, I am willing to believe, shame or fear that keeps us from making a parade of them, as awe and wonder and baffled endeavors to get our attitude towards them into expressible form. They are too elemental, too vast and overpowering in their workings to fit neatly into this busy, accounted-for, and tied-down world of daily life. They are superfluous to what we see as the higher meanings of this our life, and irritate us by their clamorous insistence and disregard for the main currents of our living. They seem irrelevant to life; or rather they overtop its bounty.

170

Their pressure to be let in is offensive, and taints and mars irrevocably what would otherwise be so pleasant and secure a life. That is, perhaps, why we call manifestations of sex activity, obscene, and of death, morbid and ghastly.

In these modern days we are adopting a healthier attitude, especially towards sex. Perhaps the rising generation will be successful in reconciling them both, and working them into our lives, where they may be seen in their right relations and proportions, and no longer the pleasure of sex and the peace of death seem an illegitimate obtrusion into life. To get command of these arch-enemies is an endeavor worthy of the moral heroes of today. We can get control, it seems, of the rest of our souls, but these always lie in wait to torment and harass us. To tame this obsession of sex and the fear of death will be a Herculean task for youth in the adventure of life. Perhaps some will succeed where we have failed. For usually when we try to tame sex, it poisons the air around us, and if we try to tame the fear of death by resigning ourselves to its inevitability, we find that we have not tamed it but only drugged it. At certain times, however, our struggles with the winged demons which they send into our minds may con-

171

stitute the most poignant incidents in our adventure of life, and add a beauty to our lives. Where they do not make for happiness, they may at least make for a deepening of knowledge and appreciation of life. Along through middle life, we shall find, perhaps, that, even if untamed, they have become our allies, and that both have lost their sting and their victory, — sex diffusing our life with a new beauty, and death with a courageous trend towards a larger life of which we shall be an integral part.

When we have acclimated ourselves to youth, suddenly death looms up as the greatest of dangers in our adventure of life. It puzzles and shocks and saddens us by its irrevocability and mystery. That we should be taken out of this world to which we are so perfectly adapted, and which we enjoy and feel intimate with, is an incredible thing. Even if we believe that we shall survive death, we know that that after-life must perforce be lived outside of this our familiar world. Reason tells us that we shall be annihilated, and yet we cannot conceive our own annihilation. We can easier imagine the time before our birth, when we were not, than the time after our death, when we shall not be. Old men find nothing very dreadful

172

in the thought of being no more, and we shall find that it is the combined notion of being annihilated, and yet of being somehow conscious of that annihilation, that terrifies us, and startles our minds sometimes in the dead of night when our spirits are sluggish and the ghoulish ideas that haunt the dimmest chambers of the mind are flitting abroad. We can reason with ourselves that if we are annihilated we shall not be conscious of it, and if we are conscious we shall not be annihilated, but this easy proof does not help us much in a practical way. We simply do not know, and all speculations seem to be equally legitimate. If we are destined to assume another form of life, no divination can prophesy for us what that life shall be.

On the face of it the soul as well as the body dies. The fate of the body we know, and it seems dreadful enough to chill the stoutest heart; and what we call our souls seem so intimately dependent upon these bodies as to be incapable of living alone. And yet somehow it is hard to stop believing in the independent soul. We can believe that the warmth dissipates, that the chemical and electrical energies of the body pass into other forms and are gradually lost in the immensity of the universe. But this wonder of consciousness,

173

which seems to hold and embrace all our thoughts
and feelings and bind them together, what can we
know of its power and permanence? In our own
limited sphere it already transcends space and
time, our imaginations triumphing over space,
and our memories and anticipations over time:
this magic power of the imagination, which transcends our feeble experience and gives ideas and
images which have not appeared directly through
the senses. We can connect this conscious life
with no other aspect of the world nor can we explain it by any of the principles which we apply
to physical things. It is the divine gift that reveals this world; why may it not reveal sometime
a far wider universe?

It is this incalculability of our conscious life
that makes its seeming end so great an adventure.
This Time which rushes past us, blotting out
everything it creates, leaving us ever suspended
on a Present, which, as we turn to look at it, has
melted away,—how are we to comprehend it? The
thin, fragile and uncertain stream of our memory
seems insufficient to give any satisfaction of permanence. I like to think of a world-memory that
retains the past. Physical things that change or
perish continue to live psychically in memory;

why may not all that passes, not only in our minds, but unknown to us, be carried along in a great world-mind of whose nature we get a dim inkling even now in certain latent mental powers of ours which are sometimes revealed, and seem to let down bars into a boundless sea of knowledge. The world is a great, rushing, irreversible life, not predestined in its workings, but free like ourselves. The accumulating past seems to cut into the future, and create it as it goes along. Nothing is then lost, and we, although we had no existence before we were born, — how could we have, since that moving Present had not created us? — would yet, having been born, continue to exist in that world-memory. We do not need to reëcho the sadness of the centuries, — "Everything passes; nothing remains!" For even if we take this world-memory at its lowest terms as a social memory, the effects of the deeds of men, for good or for evil, remain. And their words remain, the distillation of their thought and experience. This we know, and we know, moreover, that "one thing at least is certain," not that "this life dies" — for that has yet to be proved — but that "the race lives!" Nature is so careless about the individual life, so careful for the species, that it seems as if it were only the latter that counted, that her only purpose was the eternal continuation of life. And many to-day find a satisfaction for their cravings for immortality in the thought that they will live in their children and so on immortally as long as their line continues.

But we have a right to make greater hazards of faith than this. Might it not be that, although nature never purposed that the individual soul should live, man has outwitted her? He has certainly outwitted her in regard to his bodily life. There was no provision in nature for man's living by tillage of the soil and domestication of animals, or for his dwelling in houses built with tools in his hands, or for traveling at lightning speed, or for harnessing her forces to run for him the machines that should turn out the luxuries and utilities of life. All these were pure gratuities, devised by man and wrested from nature's unwilling hands. She was satisfied with primitive, animal-like man, as she is satisfied with him in some parts of the world to-day. We have simply got ahead of her. All the other animals are still under her dominion, but man has become the tool-maker and the partial master of nature herself. Although still far from thoroughly taming her, he finds in the incessant struggle his real life purpose, his inspiration, and his work, and still brighter promises for his children's children. For the race lives and takes advantage of all that has been discovered before.

Now, since nature has seemed to care as little about the continuation of life beyond death as she has of man's comfort upon earth, might it not be that, just as we have outwitted her in the physical sphere and snatched comfort and utility by our efforts, so we may, by the cultivation of our intelligence and sentiments and whole spiritual life, outwit her in this realm and snatch an immortality that she has never contemplated? She never intended that we should audaciously read her secrets and speculate upon her nature as we have done. Who knows whether, by our hardihood in exploring the uncharted seas of the life of feeling and thought, we may have over-reached her again and created a real soul, which we can project beyond death? We are provided with the raw material of our spiritual life in the world, as we are provided with the raw material to build houses, and it may be our power and our privilege to build our immortal souls here on earth, as men have built and are still building the civilization of this world of ours. This would not mean that we could all attain, any more than that all men have the creative genius or the good-will for the constructive work of civilization; there may be "real losses and real losers" in the adventure for immortality, but to the stout-hearted and the wise it will be possible. We shall need, as builders need the rules of the craft, the aid and counsel of the spiritually gifted who have gone before us. It has been no mistake that we have prized them higher even than our material builders, for we have felt instinctively the spiritual power with which they have endowed us in the contest for the mighty stake of immortality. They are helping us to it, and we have the right to rely on their visions and trusts and beliefs in this supremest and culminating episode of the adventure of life.

Are all such speculations idle and frivolous? Have they no place on the mental horizon of a youth of to-day, living in a world whose inner nature all the mighty achievements of the scientists, fruitful as they have been in their practical effects, have tended rather to obscure than to illumine? Well, a settled conviction that we live in a mechanical world, with no penumbra of mystery about us, checks the life-enhancing powers, and chills and depresses the spirit. A belief in the deadness of things actually seems to kill much of the glowing life that makes up our appreciation of art and personality in the world. The scientific philosophy is as much a matter of metaphysics, of theoretical conjecture, as the worst fanaticisms of religion. We have a right to shoot our guesses into the unknown. Life is no adventure if we let our knowledge, still so feeble and flickering, smother us. In this scientific age there is a call for youth to soar and paint a new spiritual sky to arch over our heads. If the old poetry is dead, youth must feel and write the new poetry. It has a challenge both to transcend the physical evil that taints the earth and the materialistic poison that numbs our spirits.

The wise men thought they were getting the old world thoroughly charted and explained. But there has been a spiritual expansion these recent years which has created new seas to be explored and new atmospheres to breathe. It has been discovered that the world is alive, and that discovery has almost taken away men's breaths; it has been discovered that evolution is creative and that we are real factors in that creation. After exploring the heights and depths of the stars, and getting ourselves into a state of mind where we saw the world objectively and diminished man and his interests almost to a pin-point, we have come with a rush to the realization that personality and values are, after all, the important things in a living world. And no problem of life or death can be idle. A hundred years ago it was thought chastening to the fierce pride of youth to remind it often of man's mortality. But youth today must think of everything in terms of life; yes, even of death in terms of life. We need not the chastening of pride, but the stimulation to a sense of the limitless potentialities of life. No thought or action that really enhances life is frivolous or fruitless.

What does not conduce in some way to men's interests does not enhance life. What decides in the long run whether our life will be adventurous or not is the direction and the scope of our interests. We need a livelier imaginative sympathy and interest in all that pertains to human nature and its workings. It is a good sign that youth does not need to have its attention called to the worthy and profitable interest of its own personality. It is a healthy sign that we are getting back home again to the old endeavor of "Know thyself!"

THE ADVENTURE OF LIFE

Our widening experience has shifted the centre of gravity too far from man's soul. A cultivation of the powers of one's own personality is one of the greatest needs of life, too little realized even in these assertive days, and the exercise of the personality makes for its most durable satisfactions. Men are attentive to their business affairs, but not nearly enough to their own deeper selves. If they treated their business interests as they do the interests of their personality, they would be bankrupt within a week. Few people even scratch the surface, much less exhaust the contemplation, of their own experience. Few know how to weave a philosophy of life out of it, that most precious of all possessions. And few know how to hoard their memory. For no matter what we have come through, or how many perils we have safely passed, or how imperfect and jagged — in some places perhaps irreparably — our life has been, we cannot in our heart of hearts imagine how it could have been different. As we look back on it, it slips in behind us in orderly array, and, with all its mistakes, acquires a sort of eternal fitness, and even, at times, of poetic glamour.

The things I did, I did because, after all, I am that sort of a person — that is what life is; —

and in spite of what others and what I myself might desire, it is that kind of a person that I am. The golden moments I can take a unique and splendid satisfaction in because they are my own; my realization of how poor and weak they might seem, if taken from my treasure-chest and exposed to the gaze of others, does not taint their preciousness, for I can see them in the larger light of my own life. Every man should realize that his life is an epic; unfortunately it usually takes the onlooker to recognize the fact before he does himself. We should oftener read our own epics — and write them. The world is in need of true autobiographies, told in terms of the adventure that life is. Not every one, it is said, possesses the literary gift, but what, on the other hand, is the literary gift but an absorbing interest in the personality of things, and an insight into the wonders of living? Unfortunately it is usually only the eccentric or the distinguished who reveal their inner life. Yet the epic of the humblest life, told in the light of its spiritual shocks and changes, would be enthralling in its interest. But the best autobiographers are still the masters of fiction, those wizards of imaginative sympathy, who create souls and then write their spiritual history, as those souls themselves, were they alive, could perhaps never write them. Every man, however, can cultivate this autobiographical interest in himself, and produce for his own private view a real epic of spiritual adventure. And life will be richer and more full of meaning as the story continues and life accumulates.

Life changes so gradually that we do not realize our progress. This small triumph of yesterday we fail to recognize as the summit of the mountain at whose foot we encamped several years ago in despair. We forget our hopes and wistfulness and struggles. We do not look down from the summit at the valley where we started, and thus we lose the dramatic sense of something accomplished. If a man looking back sees no mountain and valley, but only a straight level plain, it behooves him to take himself straight to some other spiritual country where there is opportunity for climbing and where five years hence will see him on a higher level, breathing purer air. Most people have no trouble in remembering their rights and their wrongs, their pretensions and their ambitions, — things so illusory that they should never even have been thought of. But to forget their progress, to forget their golden moments, their acquisitions of insight and appreciation, the charm of their friends, the sequence of their ideals, — this is indeed a deplorable aphasia! "The days that make us happy make us wise!" Happiness is too valuable to be forgotten, and who will remember yours if you forget it? It is what has made the best of you; or, if you have thrown it away from memory, what could have made you, and made you richer than you are. If you have neglected such contemplation, you are poor, and that poverty will be apparent in your daily personality.

Life in its essence is a heaping-up and accumulation of thought and insight. It should mount higher and higher, and be more potent and flowering as life is lived. If you do not keep in your memory and spirit the finer accumulations of your life, it will be as if you had only partly lived. Your living will be a travesty on life, and your progress only a dull mechanical routine. Even though your life may be outwardly routine, inwardly, as moralists have always known, it may be full of adventure. Be happy, but not too contented. Contentment may be a vice as well as a virtue; too often it is a mere cover for sluggishness, and not a sign of triumph. The mind must have a certain amount of refreshment and novelty; it will not

184

grow by staying too comfortably at home, and refusing to put itself to the trouble of travel and change. It needs to be disturbed every now and then to keep the crust from forming. People do not realize this, and let themselves become jaded and uninterested — and therefore uninteresting — when such a small touch of novelty would inspire and stimulate them. A tired interest, in a healthy mind, wakes with as quick a response to a new touch or aspect as does a thirsty flower to the rain. Too many people sit in prison with themselves until they get meagre and dull, when the door was really all the time open, and outside was freshness and green grass and the warm sun, which might have revived them and made them bright again. Listlessness in an old man or woman is often the telltale sign of such an imprisonment. Life, instead of being an accumulation of spiritual treasure, has been the squandering of its wealth, in a lapse of interest, as soon as it was earned. Even unbearable sorrow might have been the means, by a process of transmutation, of acquiring a deeper appreciation of life's truer values. But the squanderer has lost his vision, because he did not retain on the background of memory his experience, against which to contrast

185

his new reactions, and did not have the emotional image of old novelties to spur him to the apprehension and appreciation of new ones.

More amazing even than the lack of a healthy interest in their own personalities is the lack of most people of an interest, beyond one of a trivial or professional nature, in others. Our literary artists have scarcely begun to touch the resources of human ways and acts. Writers surrender reality for the sake of a plot, and in attempting to make a point, or to write adventure, squeeze out the natural traits and nuances of character and the haphazardnesses of life that are the true adventure and point. We cannot know too much about each other. All our best education comes from what people tell us or what we observe them do. We cannot endure being totally separated from others, and it is well that we cannot. For it would mean that we should have then no life above the satisfaction of our crudest material wants. Our keenest delights are based upon some manifestation or other of social life. Even gossip arises not so much from malice as from a real social interest in our neighbors; the pity of it is, of course, that to so many people it is only the misfortunes and oddities that are interesting.

THE ADVENTURE OF LIFE

Let our interests in the social world with which we come in contact be active and not passive. Let us give back in return as good an influence and as much as is given to us. Let us live so as to stimulate others, so that we call out the best powers and traits in them, and make them better than they are, because of our comprehension and inspiration. Our life is so bound up with our friends and teachers and heroes (whether present in the flesh or not), and we are so dependent upon them for nourishment and support, that we are rarely aware how little of us there would be left were they to be taken away. We are seldom conscious enough of the ground we are rooted in and the air we breathe. We can know ourselves best by knowing others. There are adventures of personality in acting and being acted upon, in studying and delighting in the ideas and folkways of people that hold much in store for those who will only seek them.

Thus in its perils and opportunities, in its satisfactions and resistances, in its gifts and responsibilities, for good or for evil, life is an adventure. In facing its evil, we shall not let it daunt or depress our spirits; we shall surrender some of our responsibility for the Universe, and face forward, working and encouraging those around us to coöperate with us and with all who suffer, in fighting preventable wrong. Death we shall transcend by interpreting everything in terms of life; we shall be victorious over it by recognizing in it an aspect of a larger life in which we are immersed. We shall accept gladly the wealth of days poured out for us. Alive, in a living world, we shall cultivate those interests and qualities which enhance life. We shall try to keep the widest possible fund of interests in order that life may mount ever richer, and not become jaded and wearied in its ebb-flow. We shall never cease to put our questions to the heart of the world, intent on tracking down the mysteries of its behavior and its meaning, using each morsel of knowledge to pry further into its secrets, and testing the tools we use by the product they create and the hidden chambers they open. To face the perils and hazards fearlessly, and absorb the satisfactions joyfully, to be curious and brave and eager, — is to know the adventure of life.

VII

SOME THOUGHTS ON RELIGION

VII

SOME THOUGHTS ON RELIGION

In youth we grow and learn and always the universe widens around us. The horizon recedes faster than we can journey towards it. There comes a time when we look back with longing to the days when everything we learned seemed a fast gaining upon the powers of darkness, and each new principle seemed to illuminate and explain an immense region of the world. We had only to keep on learning in steady progress, it seemed, until we should have dominion over the whole of it. But there came a time, perhaps, when advance halted, and our carefully ordered world began to dissipate and loose ends and fringes to appear. It became a real struggle to keep our knowledge securely boxed in our one system, indeed, in any system, as we found when we restlessly tried one dogma after another as strongboxes for our spiritual goods. Always something eluded us; it was "ever not quite." Just when we were safest, some new experience came up to be most incongruously unaccounted for. We had

191

our goods, for instance, safely stowed away in the box of "materialism," when suddenly we realized that, on its theory, our whole life might run along precisely as we see it now, we might talk and love and paint and build without a glimmer of consciousness, that wondrous stuff which is so palpably our light and our life. The materialist can see in us nothing but the inert accompaniment of our bodies, the helpless, useless, and even annoying spectators of the play of physical forces through these curious compounds of chemical elements that we call our bodies. Or if, filled with the joy of creation, we tried to pack our world into the dogma of "idealism" and see all hard material things as emanations from our spiritual self and plastic under our hand, we were brought with a shock against some tough, incorrigible fact that sobered our elation, and forced the unwilling recognition of our impotence upon us again.

It is not, however, from an excess of idealism that the world suffers to-day. But it is sick rather with the thorough-going and plausible scientific materialism with which our philosophy and literature seem to reek. Pure idealism has long ago proved too intoxicating a confirmation of our hopes and desires to seduce for long our tough-mindedness. Science has come as a challenge to both our courage and our honesty. It covertly taunts us with being afraid to face the universe as it is; if we look and are saddened, we have seemed to prove ourselves less than men. For this advance of scientific speculation has seemed only to increase the gulf between the proven and certain facts, and all the values and significances of life that our reactions to its richness have produced in us. And so incorrigibly honest is the texture of the human mind that we cannot continue to believe in and cultivate things that we no longer consider to be real. And science has undermined our faith in the reality of a spiritual world that to our forefathers was the only reality in the universe. We are so honest, however, that when the scientist relegates to a subjective shadowy realm our world of qualities and divinities, we cannot protest, but only look wistfully after the disappearing forms. A numbness has stolen over our religion, art, and literature, and the younger generation finds a chill and torpor in those interests of life that should be the highest inspiration.

Religion in these latter days becomes poetry, about which should never be asked the question,

"Is it true?" Art becomes a frivolous toy; literature a daily chronicle.

There is thus a crucial intellectual dilemma that faces us to-day. If we accept whole-heartedly the spiritual world, we seem to be false to the imposing new knowledge of science which is rapidly making the world comprehensible to us; if we accept all the claims and implications of science, we seem to trample on our own souls. Yet we feel instinctively the validity of both aspects of the world. Our solution will seem to be, then, to be content with remaining something less than monists. We must recognize that this is an infinite universe, and give up our attempt to get all our experience under one roof. Striving ever for unity, we must yet understand that this "not-quite-ness" is one of the fundamental principles of things. We can no longer be satisfied with a settlement of the dreary conflict between religion and science which left for religion only the task of making hazardous speculations which science was later to verify or cast aside, as it charted the seas of knowledge. We cannot be content with a religion which science is constantly overtaking and wiping out, as it puts its brave postulates of faith to rigorous test.

SOME THOUGHTS ON RELIGION

The only view of religion and science that will satisfy us is one that makes them each the contemplation of a different aspect of the universe, — one, an aspect of quantities and relations, the other, an aspect of qualities, ideals, and values. They may be coördinate and complementary, but they are not expressible in each others' terms. There is no question of superior reality. The blue of a flower is just as real as the ether waves which science tells us the color "really" is. Scientific and intuitive knowledge are simply different ways of appreciating an infinite universe. Scientific knowledge, for all its dogmatic claims to finality, is provisional and hypothetical. "If we live in a certain kind of a world," it says, "certain things are true." Each fact hinges upon another. Yet these correlations of the physical world are so certain and predictable that no sane mind can doubt them. On the other hand, our knowledge of qualities is direct and immediate, and seems to depend on nothing for its completeness. Yet it is so uncertain and various that no two minds have precisely the same reactions, and we do not ourselves have the same reactions at different times.

And these paradoxes give rise to the endless disputes as to which gives the more real view of

the universe in which we find ourselves living.
The matter-of-fact person takes the certainty and
lets the immediacy go; the poet and the mystic and the religious man choose the direct revelation and prize this vision far above any logical
cogency. Now it will be the task of this intellectual generation to conquer the paradoxes by
admitting the validity of both the matter-of-fact
view and the mystical. And it is the latter that
requires the present emphasis; it must be resus-
citated from the low estate into which it has
fallen. We must resist the stern arrogances of
science as vigorously as the scientist has resisted
the allurements of religion. We must remind him
that his laws are not visions of eternal truth, so
much as rough-and-ready statements of the practical nature of things, in so far as they are useful
to us for our grappling with our environment and
somehow changing it. We must demand that he
climb down out of the papal chair, and let his
learning become what it was meant to be, — the
humble servant of humanity. Truth for truth's
sake is an admirable motto for the philosopher,
who really searches to find the inner nature of
things. But the truth of science is for use's sake.
To seek for physical truth which is irrelevant to

human needs and purposes is as purely futile an intellectual gymnastic as the logical excesses of the schoolmen. The scientist is here to tell us the practical workings of the forces and elements of the world; the philosopher, mystic, artist, and poet are here to tell us of the purposes and meanings of the world as revealed directly, and to show us the ideal aspect through their own clear fresh vision.

That vision, however, must be controlled and enriched by the democratic experience of their fellow men; their ideal must be to reveal meanings that cannot be doubted by the normal soul, in the same way that scientific formulations cannot be doubted by the normal mind. It is here that we have a quarrel with old religion and old poetry, that the vision which it brings us is not sufficiently purged of local discolorations or intellectualistic taints. But it is not a quarrel with religion and poetry as such; this age thirsts for a revelation of the spiritual meanings of the wider world that has been opened to us, and the complex and baffling anomalies that seem to confront us. It is our imperative duty to reëmphasize the life of qualities and ideals, to turn again our gaze to that aspect of the world from which men have

always drawn what gave life real worth and reinstate those spiritual things whose strength advancing knowledge has seemed to sap. There is
room for a new idealism, but an idealism that
sturdily keeps its grip on the real, that grapples
with the new knowledge and with the irrevocable
loss of much of the old poetry and many of the old
values, and wrests out finer qualities and a nobler
spiritual life than the world has yet seen. It is
not betrayal of our integrity to believe that the
desires and interests of men, their hopes and fears
and creative imaginings, are as real as any atoms
or formulas.

Now the place of religion in this new idealism
will be the same place that its essential spirit has
always held in the spiritual life of men. Religion
is our sense of the quality of the universe itself,
the broadest, profoundest, and most constant of
our intuitions. Men have always felt that, outside of the qualities of concrete things, there lay
a sort of infinite quality that they could identify
with the spirit of the universe, and they have
called it God. To this quality men have always
responded, and that response and appreciation
is religion. To appreciate this cosmic quality is
to be religious, and to express that appreciation

is to worship. Religion is thus as much and eternally a part of life as our senses themselves; the only justification for making away with religion would be an event that would make away with our senses. The scientist must always find it difficult to explain why, if man's mind, as all agree that it did, developed in adaptation to his environment, it should somehow have become adapted so perfectly to a spiritual world of qualities and poetic interpretation of phenomena, and not to the world of atomic motion and mechanical law which scientific philosophy assures us is the "real" world. Our minds somehow adapted themselves, not to the hard world of fact, but to a world of illusion, which had not the justification of being even practically useful or empirically true. If the real world is mechanical, we should have a right to expect the earliest thinking to be scientific, and the spiritual life to come in only after centuries of refinement of thought. But the first reactions of men were of course purely qualitative, and it is only within the last few minutes of cosmic time that we have known of the quantitative relations of things. Is it hard, then, to believe that, since we and the world have grown up together, there must be some subtle correla-

199

tion between it and the values and qualities that we feel, that our souls must reflect — not faithfully, perhaps, because warped by a thousand alien compelling physical forces, and yet somehow indomitably — a spiritual world that is perhaps even more real, because more immediate and constant, than the physical? We may partially create it, but we partially reflect it too.

That cosmic quality we feel as personality. Not artificial or illusive is this deeply rooted anthropomorphic sense which has always been at the bottom of man's religious consciousness. We are alive, and we have a right to interpret the world as living; we are persons, and we have a right to interpret the world in terms of personality. In all religions, through the encrustations of dogma and ritual, has been felt that vital sense of the divine personality, keeping clean and sweet the life of man. The definite appeal of the Church, in times like these, when the external props fall away, is to the incarnation of the divine personality, and the ideal of character deduced from it as a pattern for life. This is the religion of ordinary people to-day; it has' been the heart of Christianity for nineteen hundred years. Our feeling of this cosmic quality may be vague

or definite, diffused or crystallized, but to those
of us who sense behind our pulsing life a mystery
which perplexes sobers, and elevates us, that
quality forms a permanent scenic background for
our life.

To feel this cosmic quality of a divine personality, in whom we live, move, and have our being,
is to know religion. The ordinary world we live
in is incurably dynamic; we are forced to think
and act in terms of energy and change and constant rearrangement and flux of factors and elements. And we live only as we give ourselves up
to that stream and play of forces. Throughout
all the change, however, there comes a sense of
this eternal quality. In the persistence of our own
personality, the humble fragment of a divine personality, we get the pattern of its permanence.
The Great Companion is ever with us, silently
ratifying our worthy deeds and tastes and responses. The satisfactions of our spiritual life, of
our judgments and appreciations of morality and
art and any kind of excellence, come largely from
this subtle corroboration that we feel from some
unseen presence wider than ourselves. It accom-
panies not a part but the whole of our spiritual
life, silently strengthening our responses to per-

sonality and beauty, our sense of irony, the refinement of our taste, sharpening our moral judgment, elevating our capacities for happiness, filling ever richer our sense of the worth of life. And this cosmic influence in which we seem to be immersed we can no more lose or doubt — after we have once felt the rush of time past us, seen a friend die, or brooded on the bitter thought of our personal death, felt the surge of forces of life and love, wondered about consciousness, been melted before beauty — than we can lose or doubt ourselves. The wonder of it is exhaustless, — the beneficence over whose workings there yet breathes an inexorable sternness, the mystery of time and death, the joy of beauty and creative art and sex, and sheer consciousness.

Against this scenic background, along this deep undercurrent of feeling, our outward, cheerful, settled, and orderly life plays its part. That life is no less essential; we must be willing to see life in two aspects, the world as deathless yet ever-creative, evolution yet timeless eternity. To be religious is to turn our gaze away from the dynamic to the static and the permanent, away from the stage to the scenic background of our lives. Religion cannot, therefore, be said to have much of a place in our activity of life, except as it fixes the general emotional tone. We have no right to demand that it operate practically, nor can we call altruistic activity, and enthusiasm for a noble cause, religion. Moral action is really more a matter of social psychology than of religion. All religions have been ethical only as a secondary consideration. Religion in and for itself is something else; we can enjoy it only by taking, as it were, the moral holiday into its regions when we are weary of the world of thinking and doing. It is a land to retreat into when we are battered and degraded by the dynamic world about us, and require rest and recuperation. It is constantly there behind us, but to live in it always is to take a perpetual holiday.

At all times we may have its beauty with us, however, as we may have prospects of far mountains and valleys. As we go in the morning to work in the fields, religion is this enchanting view of the mountains, inspiring us and lifting our hearts with renewed vigor. Through all the long day's work we feel their presence with us, and have only to turn around to see them shining splendidly afar with hope and kindliness. Even the austerest summits are warm in the afternoon sun. Yet if we gaze at them all day long, we shall accomplish no work. Nor shall we finish our allotted task if we succumb to their lure and leave our fields to travel towards them. As we return home weary at night, the mountains are still there to refresh and cheer us with their soft colors and outline blended in the purple light. When our task is entirely done, it has been our eternal hope to journey to those far mountains and valleys; if this is not to be, at least their glorious view will be the last to fall upon us as we close our eyes. But we know that, whatever happens, if we have done our work well, have performed faithfully our daily tasks of learning to control and manage and make creative the tough soil of this material world in which we find ourselves, if we have neither allowed its toughness to distract us from the beauty of the eternal background, nor let those far visions slow down the wheels of life, distract us from our work, or blur our thought and pale by their light the other qualities and beauties around us — we shall attain what is right for us when we lay down our tools. In a living world, death can be no more than an apparition.

VIII

THE MYSTIC TURNED RADICAL

VIII

THE MYSTIC TURNED RADICAL

THE mystical temperament is little enough popular in this workaday modern world of ours. The mystic, we feel, comes to us discounted from the start; he should in all decency make constant apologies for his existence. In a practical age of machinery he is an anomaly, an anachronism. He must meet the direct challenge of the scientist, who guards every approach to the doors of truth and holds the keys of its citadel. Any thinker who gets into the fold by another way is a thief and a robber.

The mystic must answer that most heinous of all charges, — of being unscientific. By tradition he is even hostile to science. For his main interest is in wonder, and science by explaining things attacks the very principle of his life. It not only diminishes his opportunities for wonder, but threatens to make him superfluous by ultimately explaining everything.

The scientist may say that there is no necessary antithesis between explanation and that beautiful romance of thought we call wonder. The savage, who can explain nothing, is the very creature who has no wonder at all. Everything is equally natural to him. Only a mind that has acquaintance with laws of behavior can be surprised at events.

The wonder of the scientist, however, although it be of a more robust, tough-minded variety, is none the less wonder. A growing acquaintance with the world, an increasing at-homeness in it, is not necessarily incompatible with an ever-increasing marvel both at the beautiful fitness of things and the limitless field of ignorance and mystery beyond. So the modern mystic must break with his own tradition if he is to make an appeal to this generation, and must recognize that the antithesis between mystic and scientific is not an eternally valid one.

It is just through realization of this fact that Maeterlinck, the best of modern mystics, makes his extraordinary appeal. For, as he tells us, the valid mystery does not begin at the threshold of knowledge but only after we have exhausted our resources of knowing. His frank and genuine acceptance of science thus works out a *modus vivendi* between the seen and the unseen. It allows many of us who have given our allegiance to science to hail him gladly as a prophet who supplements the work of the wise men of scientific research, without doing violence to our own consciences. For the world is, in spite of its scientific clamor, still far from ready really to surrender itself to prosaicness. It is still haunted with the dreams of the ages — dreams of short roads to truth, visions of finding the Northwest passage to the treasures of the Unseen. Only we must go as far as possible along the traveled routes of science.

Maeterlinck is thus not anti-scientific or pseudo-scientific, but rather sub-scientific. He speaks of delicately felt and subtle influences and aspects of reality that lie beneath the surface of our lives, of forces and shadows that cannot be measured quantitatively or turned into philosophical categories. Or we may say that he is ultra-scientific. As science plods along, opening up the dark wilderness, he goes with the exploring party, throwing a search-light before them; flickering enough and exasperatingly uncertain at times, but sufficiently constant to light up the way, point out a path, and give us confidence that the terrors before us are not so formidable as we have feared. His influence on our time is so great because we believe that he is a seer, a man with knowledge of

209

things hidden from our eyes. We go to him as to a spiritual clairvoyant, — to have him tell us where to find the things our souls have lost.

But the modern mystic must not only recognize the scientific aspect of the age, — he must feel the social ideal that directs the spiritual energies of the time. It is the glory of Maeterlinck's mysticism that it has not lingered in the depths of the soul, but has passed out to illuminate our thinking in regard to the social life about us. The growth of this duality of vision has been with him a long evolution. His early world was a shadowy, intangible thing. As we read the early essays, we seem to be constantly hovering on the verge of an idea, just as when we read the plays we seem to be hovering on the verge of a passion. This long brooding away from the world, however, was fruitful and momentous. The intense gaze inward trained the eye, so that when the mists cleared away and revealed the palpitating social world about him, his insight into its meaning was as much more keen and true than our own as had been his sense of the meaning of the individual soul. The light he turns outward to reveal the meaning of social progress is all the whiter for having burned so long within.

THE MYSTIC TURNED RADICAL

In the essay on "Our Social Duty," the clearest and the consummate expression of this new outward-look, there are no contaminating fringes of vague thought; all is clear white light. With the instinct of the true radical, the poet has gone to the root of the social attitude. Our duty as members of society is to be radical, he tells us. And not only that, but an excess of radicalism is essential to the equilibrium of life. Society so habitually thinks on a plane lower than is reasonable that it behooves us to think and to hope on an even higher plane than seems to be reasonable. This is the overpoweringly urgent philosophy of radicalism. It is the beautiful courage of such words that makes them so vital an inspiration.

It is the sin of the age that nobody dares to be anything to too great a degree. We may admire extremists in principle, but we take the best of care not to imitate them ourselves. Who in America would even be likely to express himself as does Maeterlinck in this essay? Who of us would dare follow the counsel? Of course we can plead extenuation. In Europe the best minds are thinking in terms of revolution still, while in America our radicalism is still simply amateurish and incompetent.

To many of us, then, this call of Maeterlinck's to the highest of radicalisms will seem irrelevant; this new social note which appears so strongly in all his later work will seem a deterioration from the nobler mysticism of his earlier days. But rather should it be viewed as the fruit of matured insight. There has been no decay, no surrender. It is the same mysticism, but with the direction of the vision altered. This essay is the expression of the clearest vision that has yet penetrated our social confusion, the sanest and highest ideal that has been set before progressive minds. It may be that its utter fearlessness, its almost ascetic detachment from the matter-of-fact things of political life, its clear cold light of conviction and penetration, may repel some whose hearts have been warmed by Maeterlinck's subtle revelations of the spiritual life. They may reproach him because it has no direct bearings on the immediate practical social life; it furnishes no weapon of reform, no tool with which to rush out and overthrow some vested abuse. But to the traveler lost in the wood the one thing needful is a pole-star to show him his direction. The star is unapproachable, serene, cold, and lofty. But although he cannot touch it, or utilize it directly to extend his comfort and progress, it is the most useful of all things to him. It fills his heart with a great hope; it coördinates his aimless wanderings and gropings, and gives meaning and purpose to his course.

So a generation lost in a chaos of social change can find in these later words of Maeterlinck a polestar and a guide. They do for the social life of man what the earlier essays did for the individual. They endow it with values and significances that will give steadfastness and resource to his vision as he looks out on the great world of human progress, and purpose and meaning to his activity as he looks ahead into the dim world of the future.

IX

SEEING, WE SEE NOT

IX

SEEING, WE SEE NOT

IT is a mere superstition, Maeterlinck tells us in one of his beautiful essays, that there is anything irrevocable about the past. On the contrary, we are constantly rearranging it, revising it, remaking it. For it is only in our memory that it exists, and our conception of it changes as the loose fringes of past events are gathered up into a new meaning, or when a sudden fortune lights up a whole series in our lives, and shows us, stretching back in orderly array and beautiful significance, what we had supposed in our blindness to be a sad and chaotic welter. It is no less a superstition to suppose that we have a hand in making the present. The present, like the past, is always still to be made; indeed, must wait its turn, so to speak, to be seen in its full meaning until after the past itself has been remoulded and reconstituted. It is depressing to think that we do not know our own time, that the events we look upon have a permanent value far different from the petty one that we endow them with, that they fit into a larger whole of which we see only a dim fraction — and that the least important because the seed of something that shall come much later into full fruition. Must our short life pass away without knowledge or vision of the majestic processes which are unfolding themselves under our very eyes, while we have wasted our admiration and distorted our purpose by striving to interpret the ephemeral, that is gone as soon as we? Even the wisest among us can see with but a dim eye into the future, and make rather a lucky guess at its potentialities than a true prophecy based on a realization of the real tendencies of the time. It is only the Past that we really make. And this may account for our love of it. This fragile thing of tradition that we have so carefully constructed and so lovingly beautified, this artistic creation of a whole people or race, becomes most naturally the object of our tenderest solicitude. Any attack upon it that suggests a marring of its golden beauty, any new proposal that threatens to render it superfluous, elicits the outraged cry of anger, the passionate defense, of the mother protecting her child. For the Past is really the child of the Present. We are the authors of its being, and upon it we lavish all our thoughts, our interest and our delight. And even our hopes are centred in the Past, for the most enthusiastic among us can do no more than hope that something worth while will come out of the Past to nourish us in the approaching Present. Concern for the Future is so new a thing in human history that we are hardly yet at home with the feeling. Perhaps, if we thought more about what was before us, we should come to know more about it. Meanwhile our only consolation is that if *we* cannot see, neither did the generations that were before us. And we have the advantage of *knowing* that we do not see, while they did not care about their ignorance at all.

We have constantly to check ourselves in reading history with the remembrance that, to the actors in the drama, events appeared very differently from the way they appear to us. We know what they were doing far better than they knew themselves. We are in the position of the novel reader who looks, before he begins to read, to see how the plot turns out. This orderly and dramatic chronicle of history that thrills us as we read has only been orderly and dramatic to readers of the present time, who can see the *dénouement* of the story. History is peculiarly the creation of the present. Even the great men of the past are largely

219

the agglomerations of centuries of hero-worship. Genius is as much a slow accretion of the ages as an endowment of man. Few great poets were seen in the full glory of their superhuman capacity by their fellows. Contemporary opinion of the great has been complimentary but seldom excessively laudatory, and there are sad instances of the decay and deflation of a supernatural personality through the smooth, gentle, imperceptibly creeping oblivion of the centuries.

We rarely see what is distinctive in our own time. The city builders of the West are quite unconscious of the fact that they are leaving behind them imperishable and mighty memorials of themselves. Few of the things that we admire now will be considered by posterity as noteworthy and distinctive of our age. All depends on the vitality of our customs and social habits, and some show as high a mortality as others do a stubborn tenacity of life. What we are witnessing is a gigantic struggle of customs and ideas to survive and propagate their kind. The means of subsistence is limited; it is impossible that all should be able to live. The fascinating problem for the social philosopher is which of these beliefs and tendencies will prove strong enough to overcome their rivals and make their stock a permanent type. How many of the fads and brilliant theories and new habits of thought and taste will be able to maintain their place in the world? If we could discern them, we should know the distinction of our age. Definite epochs of the past we distinguish and celebrate because they contained the germs of ideas or the roots of institutions that still survive among us, or customs and habits of thought that flourished in them with great brilliancy but have now utterly passed away. Now these beginnings are quite too subtle for us to see in our contemporary life, and there are so many brilliancies that it is impossible to pick out with any definiteness the things which have power to project themselves into the future, and cast a broad trail of light back to our age. Most of those very things that seem to us imperishable will be the ones to fade, — fade, indeed, so gradually that they will not even be missed. It is this gradual disappearance that gives the most thorough oblivion. History remembers only the brilliant failures and the brilliant successes.

We are fond of calling this an age of transition, but if we trace history back we find that practically every age — at least for many centuries — has

been an age of transition. If we must set a start-
ing-point from which we have been moving, the
social philosopher will be inclined to place it about
the beginning of the sixteenth century. If we
have been in transition for four hundred years, it
seems almost time to settle down from this wild
ferment of beliefs and discoveries that has kept
the world's mind in constant turmoil since the
time of the Renaissance. There are signs that
such a crystallization is taking place. We are
weeding out our culture, and casting aside the
classical literature that was the breeding-ground
for the old ideas. We have achieved as yet little
to take its place. Most of the modern literature
is rather a restless groping about in the dark for
new modes of thinking and new principles of life,
and thus far it hardly seems to have grasped the
robust and vital in the new to any appreciable
extent. One can hardly believe that this morbid virus that is still working with undiminished
vigor and deadly effect will succeed in making
itself the dominant note in European literature
for the next five hundred years. One hates to
think that our posterity is to be doomed to
torture itself into appreciating our feverish modern art and music, and learn to rank the wild

complexities of Strauss with the sublimities of Beethoven. Shall we be sure that the conquest of the air is finally achieved and a third dimension added to man's traveling, or is it all simply another daring and brilliant stab at the impossible, another of those blasphemies against nature which impious man is constantly striving to commit? There are few signs of the Socialistic State, but who knows what births of new institutions, of which we are now quite unaware, future ages will see to have been developing in our very midst? Is religion doomed, or is it merely being transformed, so that we shall be seen to have been creating amid all our indifference a new type and a new ideal? Will our age actually be distinctive as the era of the Dawn of Peace, or will the baby institution of arbitration disappear before a crude and terrible reality? Are we progressing, or shall we seem to have sown the seeds of world decay in this age of ours, and at a great crisis in history let slip another opportunity to carry mankind to a higher social level? It is maddening to the philosopher to think how long he will have to live to find an answer to these questions. He wants to know, but in the present all he can do is to guess at random. Not immortality, but an opportunity to wake up every hundred years or so to see how the world is progressing, may well be his desire and his dream. Such an immortality may be incredible, but it is the only form which has ever proved satisfactory, or ever will, to the rational man.

X

THE EXPERIMENTAL LIFE

X

THE EXPERIMENTAL LIFE

IT is good to be reasonable, but too much rationality puts the soul at odds with life. For rationality implies an almost superstitious reliance on logical proofs and logical motives, and it is logic that life mocks and contradicts at every turn. The most annoying people in the world are those who demand reasons for everything, and the most discouraging are those who map out ahead of them long courses of action, plan their lives, and systematically in the smallest detail of their activity adapt means to ends. Now the difficulty with all the prudential virtues is that they imply a world that is too good to be true. It would be pleasant to have a world where cause and effect interlocked, where we could see the future, where virtue had its reward, and our characters and relations with other people and the work we wish to do could be planned out with the same certainty with which cooks plan a meal. But we know that that is not the kind of a world we actually live in. Perhaps men have thought that, by cultivating the rational virtues and laying emphasis on prudence and forethought, they could bend the stubborn constitution of things to meet their ideals. It has always been the fashion to insist, in spite of all the evidence, that the world was in reality a rational place where certain immutable moral principles could be laid down with the same certainty of working that physical laws possess. It has always been represented that the correct procedure of the moral life was to choose one's end or desire, to select carefully all the means by which that end could be realized, and then, by the use of the dogged motive force of the will, to push through the plans to completion. In the homilies on success, it has always been implied that strength of will was the only requisite. Success became merely a matter of the ratio between the quantity of effort and will-power applied, and the number of obstacles to be met. If one failed, it was because the proper amount of effort had not been applied, or because the plans had not been properly constructed. The remedy was automatically to increase the effort or rationalize the plans. Life was considered to be a battle, the strategy of which a general might lay out beforehand, an engagement in which he might plan and anticipate to the minutest detail the movement of his forces and the disposition of the enemy. But one does not have to live very long to see that this belief in the power and the desirability of controlling things is an illusion. Life works in a series of surprises. One's powers are given in order that one may be alert and ready, resourceful and keen. The interest of life lies largely in its adventurousness, and not in its susceptibility to orderly mapping. The enemy rarely comes up from the side the general has expected; the battle is usually fought out on vastly different lines from those that have been carefully foreseen and rationally organized. And similarly in life do complex forces utterly confound and baffle our best laid plans.

Our strategy, unless it is open to instant correction, unless it is flexible, and capable of infinite resource and modification, is a handicap rather than an aid in the battle of life. In spite of the veracious accounts of youths hewing their way to success as captains of industry or statesmen, with their eye singly set on a steadfast purpose, we may be sure that life seldom works that way. It is not so tractable and docile, even to the strongest. The rational ideal is one of those great moral hypocrisies which every one preaches and no one practices, but which we all believe with superstitious reverence, and which we take care shall be proven erroneous by no stubborn facts of life. Better that the facts should be altered than that the moral tradition should die!

One of its evil effects is the compressing influence it has on many of us. Recognizing that for us the world is an irrational place, we are willing to go on believing that there are at least some gifted beings who are proving the truth and vindicating the eternal laws of reason. We join willingly the self-stigmatized ranks of the incompetent and are content to shine feebly in the reflected light of those whose master wills and power of effort have brought them through in rational triumph to their ends. The younger generation is coming very seriously to doubt both the practicability and worth of this rational ideal. They do not find that the complex affairs of either the world or the soul work according to laws of reason. The individual as a member of society is at the mercy of great social laws that regulate his fortune for him, construct for him his philosophy of life, and dictate to him his ways of making a living. As an individual soul, he is the creature of impulses and instincts which he does not create and which seem to lie quite outside the reach of his rational will. Looked at from this large social viewpoint, his will appears a puny affair indeed. There seems little room left in which to operate, either in the sphere of society or in his own spiritual life. That little of free-will, however, which there is, serves for our human purposes. It must be our care simply that we direct it wisely; and the rational ideal is not the wisest way of directing it. The place of our free will in the scheme of life is not to furnish driving, but *directing* power. The engineer could never create the power that drives his engine, but he can direct it into the channels where it will be useful and creative. The superstition of the strong will has been almost like an attempt to create power, something the soul could never do. The rational ideal has too often been a mere challenge to attain the unattainable. It has ended in futility or failure.

This superstition comes largely from our incorrigible habit of looking back over the past, and putting purpose into it. The great man looking back over his career, over his ascent from the humble level of his boyhood to his present power and riches, imagines that that ideal success was in his mind from his earliest years. He sees a progress, which was really the happy seizing of fortunate opportunities, as the carrying-out of a fixed purpose. But the purpose was not there at the beginning; it is the crowning touch added to the picture, which completes and satisfies our age-long hunger for the orderly and correct. But we all, rich and poor, successful and unsuccessful, live from hand to mouth. We all alike find life at the beginning a crude mass of puzzling possibilities. All of us, unless we inherit a place in the world, — and then we are only half alive, — have the same precarious struggle to get a foothold. The difference is in the fortune of the foothold, and not in our private creation of any mystical force of will. It is a question of happy occasions of exposure to the right stimulus that will develop our powers at the right time. The capacity alone is sterile; it needs the stimulus to fertilize it and produce activity and success. The part that our free will can play is to expose ourselves consciously to the stimulus; it cannot create it or the capacity, but it can bring them together.

In other words, for the rational ideal we must substitute the experimental ideal. Life is not a campaign of battle, but a laboratory where its possibilities for the enhancement of happiness and the realization of ideals are to be tested and observed. We are not to start life with a code of its laws in our pocket, with its principles of activity already learned by heart, but we are to discover those principles as we go, by conscientious experiment. Even those laws that seem incontrovertible we are to test for ourselves, to see whether they are thoroughly vital to our own experience and our own genius. We are animals, and our education in life is, after all, different only in degree, and not in kind, from that of the monkey who learns the trick of opening his cage. To get out of his cage, the monkey must find and open a somewhat complicated latch. How does he set about it? He blunders around for a long time, without method or purpose, but with the waste of an enormous amount of energy. At length he accidentally strikes the right catch, and the door flies open. Our procedure in youth is little different. We feel a vague desire to expand, to get out of our cage, and liberate our dimly felt powers. We blunder around for a time, until we accidentally put ourselves in a situation where some capacity is touched, some latent energy liberated, and the direction set for us, along which we have only to move to be free and successful. We will be hardly human if we do not look back on the process and congratulate ourselves on our tenacity and purpose and strong will. But of course the thing was wholly irrational. There were neither plans nor purposes, perhaps not even discoverable effort. For when we found the work that we did best, we found also that we did it easiest. And the outlines of the most dazzling career are little different. Until habits were formed or prestige acquired which could float these successful geniuses, their life was but the resourceful seizing of opportunity, the utilization, with a minimum of purpose or effort, of the promise of the passing moment. They were living the experimental life, aided by good fortune and opportunity.

Now the youth brought up to the strictly rational ideal is like the animal who tries to get out of his cage by going straight through the bars. The duck, beating his wings against his cage, is a symbol of the highest rationality. His logic is plain, simple, and direct. He is in the cage; there is the free world outside; nothing but the bars separate them. The problem is simply to fortify his will and effort and make them so strong that they will overcome the resistance of the cage. His error evidently lies not in his method, but in his estimation of the strength of the bars. But youth is no wiser; it has no data upon which to estimate either its own strength or the strength of its obstacles. It counts on getting out through its own self-reliant strength and will. Like the duck, "impossible" is a word not found in its vocabulary. And like the duck, it too often dashes out its spirit against the bars of circumstance. How often do we see young people, brought up with the old philosophy that nothing was withheld from those who wanted and worked for things with sufficient determination, beating their ineffectual wings against their bars, when perhaps in another direction the door stands open that would lead to freedom!

We do not hear enough of the tragedies of misplaced ambition. When the plans of the man of will and determination fail, and he inexorable forces of life twist his purposes aside from their end, he is sure to suffer the prostration of failure. His humiliation, too, is in proportion to the very strength of his will. It is the burden of defeat, or at best the sting of petty success, that crushes men, and crushes them all the more thoroughly if they have been brought up to believe in the essential rationality of the world and the power of will and purpose. It is not that they have aimed too high, but that they have aimed in the wrong direction. They have not set out experimentally to find the work to which their powers were adapted, they did not test coolly and impartially the direction in which their achievement lay. They forgot that, though faith may remove mountains, the will alone is not able. There is an urgency on every man to develop his powers to the fullest capacity, but he is not called upon to develop those that he does not possess. The will cannot create talent or opportunity. The wise man is he who has the clear vision to discern the one, and the calm patience to await the other. Will, without humor and irony and a luminous knowledge of one's self, is likely to drive one to dash one's brains out against a stone wall. The world is too full of people with nothing except a will. The mistake of youth is to believe that the philosophy of experimentation is enervating. They want to attack life frontally, to win by the boldness of their attack, or by the exceeding excellence of their rational plans and purposes. But therein comes a time when they learn perhaps that it is better to take life not with their naked fists, but more scientifically, — to stand with mind and soul alert, ceaselessly testing and criticizing, taking and rejecting, poised for opportunity, and sensitive to all good influences.

The experimental life does not put one at the mercy of chance. It is rather the rational mind that is constantly being shocked and deranged by circumstances. But the dice of the experimenter are always loaded. For he does not go into an enterprise, spiritual or material, relying simply on his reason and will to pull him through. He asks himself beforehand whether something good is not sure to come whichever way the dice fall, or at least whether he can bear the event of failure, whether his spirit can stand it if the experiment ends in humiliation and barrenness. It is surprising how many seeming disasters one finds one can bear in this anticipatory look; the tension of the failure is relieved, anyhow. By looking ahead, one has insured one's self up to the limit of the venture, and one cannot lose. But to the man with the carefully planned campaign, every step is crucial. If all does not turn out exactly as he intends, he is ruined. He thinks he insures himself by the excellence of his designs and the craftiness of his skill. But he insures himself by the strange method of putting all his eggs in one basket. He thinks, of course, he has arranged his plans so that, if they fall, the universe falls with them. But when the basket breaks, and the universe does not fall, his ruin is complete.

Ambition and the rational ideal seem to be only disastrous; if unsuccessful, they produce misanthropists; if successful, beings that prey upon their fellow men. Too much rationality makes a man mercenary and calculating. He has too much at stake in everything he does to know that calm disinterestedness of spirit which is the mark of the experimental attitude towards life. Our attitude towards our personal affairs, material and spiritual, should be like the interest we take in sports and games. The sporting interest is one secret of a healthy attitude towards life. The detached enthusiasm it creates is a real ingredient of happiness. The trouble with the rational man is that he has bet on the game. If his side wins, there is a personal reward for him; if it loses, he himself suffers a loss. He cannot know the true sporting interest which is unaffected by considerations of the end, and views the game as the thing, and not the outcome. To the experimental attitude,

238

failure means nothing beyond a shade of regret or chagrin. Whether we win or lose, something has been learned, some insight and appreciation of the workings of others or of ourselves. We are ready and eager to begin another game; defeat has not dampened our enthusiasm. But if the man who has made the wager loses, he has lost, too, all heart for playing. Or, if he does try again, it is not for interest in the game, but with a redoubled intensity of self-interest to win back what he has lost. With the sporting interest, one looks on one's relations with others, on one's little rôle in the world, in the same spirit that we look on a political contest, where we are immensely stirred by the clash of issues and personalities, but where we know that the country will run on in about the same way, whoever is elected. This knowledge does not work against our interest in the struggle itself, nor in the outcome. It only insures us against defeat. It makes life livable by endowing us with disinterestedness. If we lose, why, better luck next time, or, at worst, is not losing a part of life?

The experimenter with life, then, must go into his laboratory with the mind of the scientist. He has nothing at stake except the discovery of the truth, and he is willing to work carefully and methodically and even cold-bloodedly in eliciting it from the tangled skein of phenomena. But it is exactly in this cheerful, matter-of-fact way that we are never willing to examine our own personalities and ideas. We take ourselves too seriously, and handle our tastes and enthusiasms as gingerly as if we feared they would shrivel away at the touch. We perpetually either underestimate or overestimate our powers and worth, and suffer such losses on account of the one and humiliations on account of the other, as serve to unbalance our knowledge of ourselves, and discourage attempts to find real guiding principles of our own or others' actions. We need this objective attitude of the scientist. We must be self-conscious with a detached self-consciousness, treating ourselves as we treat others, experimenting to discover our possibilities and traits, testing ourselves with situations, and gradually building up a body of law and doctrine for ourselves, a real morality that will have far more worth and power and virtue than all that has been tried and tested before by no matter how much of alien human experience. We must start our quest with no prepossessions, with no theory of what ought to happen when we expose ourselves to certain stimuli. It is our business to see what does happen, and then act accordingly. If the electrical experimenter started with a theory that like magnetic poles attract each other, he would be shocked to discover that they actually repelled each other. He might even set it down to some inherent depravity of matter. But if his theory was not a prejudice but a hypothesis, he would find it possible to revise it quickly when he saw how the poles actually behaved. And he would not feel any particular chagrin or humiliation.

But we usually find it so hard to revise our theories about ourselves and each other. We hold them as prejudices and not as hypotheses, and when the facts of life seem to disprove them, we either angrily clutch at our theories and snarl in defiance, or we pull them out of us with such a wrench that they draw blood. The scientist's way is to start with a hypothesis and then to proceed to verify it by experiment. Similarly ought we to approach life and test all our hypotheses by experience. Our methods have been too rigid. We have started with moral dogmas, and when life obstinately refused to ratify them, we have railed at it, questioned its sincerity, instead of adopting some new hypothesis, which more nearly fitted our experience, and testing it until we hit on the principle which explained our workings to ourselves. The common-sense, rule-of-thumb morality which has come down to us is no more valid than the common-sense, scientific observation that the sun goes round the earth. We can rely no longer on the loose gleanings of homely proverb and common sense for our knowledge of personality and human nature and life.

If we do not adopt the experimental life, we are still in bondage to convention. To learn of life from others' words is like learning to build a steam-engine from books in the class-room. We may learn of principles in the spiritual life that have proven true for millions of men, but even these we must test to see if they hold true for our individual world. We can never attain any self-reliant morality if we allow ourselves to be hypnotized by fixed ideas of what is good or bad. No matter how good our principles, our devotion to morality will be mere lip-service unless each belief is individually tested, and its power to work vitally in our lives demonstrated.

But this moral experimentation is not the mere mechanical repetition of the elementary student in the laboratory, who makes simple experiments which are sure to come out as the law predicts. The laws of personality and life are far more complex, and each experiment discovers something really novel and unique. The spiritual world is ever-creative; the same experiments may turn out differently for different experimenters, and yet they may both be right. In the spiritual experimental life, we must have the attitude of the scientist, but we are able to surpass him in daring and boldness. We can be certain of a physical law that as it has worked in the past, so it will work in the future. But of a spiritual law we have no such guarantee. This it is that gives the zest of perpetual adventure to the moral life. Human nature is an exhaustless field for investigation and experiment. It is inexhaustible in its richness and variety.

The old rigid morality, with its emphasis on the prudential virtues, neglected the fundamental fact of our irrationality. It believed that if we only knew what was good, we would do it. It was therefore satisfied with telling us what was good, and expecting us automatically to do it. But there was a hiatus somewhere. For we do not do what we want to, but what is easiest and most natural for us to do, and if it is easy for us to do the wrong thing, it is that that we will do. We are creatures of instincts and impulses that we do not set going. And education has never taught us more than very imperfectly how to train these impulses in accordance with our worthy desires. Instead of endeavoring to cure this irrationality by directing our energy into the channel of experimentation, it has worked along the lines of greatest resistance, and held up an ideal of inhibition and restraint. We have been alternately exhorted to stifle our bad impulses, and to strain and struggle to make good our worthy purposes and ambitions. Now the irrational man is certainly a slave to his impulses, but is not the rational man a slave to his motives and reasons? The rational ideal has made directly for inflexibility of character, a deadening conservatism that is unable to adapt itself to situations, or make allowance for the changes and ironies of life. It has riveted the moral life to logic, when it should have been yoked up with sympathy. The logic of the heart is usually better than the logic of the head, and the consistency of sympathy is superior as a rule for life to the consistency of the intellect.

Life is a laboratory to work out experiments in

244

living. That same freedom which we demand for ourselves, we must grant to every one. Instead of falling with our spite upon those who vary from the textbook rules of life, we must look upon their acts as new and very interesting hypotheses to be duly tested and judged by the way they work when carried out into action. Nonconformity, instead of being irritating and suspicious, as it is now to us, will be distinctly pleasurable, as affording more material for our understanding of life and our formulation of its satisfying philosophy. The world has never favored the experimental life. It despises poets, fanatics, prophets, and lovers. It admires physical courage, but it has small use for moral courage. Yet it has always been those who experimented with life, who formed their philosophy of life as a crystallization out of that experimenting, who were the light and life of the world. Causes have only finally triumphed when the rational "gradual progress" men have been overwhelmed. Better crude irrationality than the rationality that checks hope and stifles faith.

In place, then, of the rational or the irrational life, we preach the experimental life. There is much chance in the world, but there is also a modicum of free will, and it is this modicum that

we exploit to direct our energies. Recognizing the
precariousness and haphazardness of life, we can
yet generalize out of our experience certain prob-
abilities and satisfactions that will serve us as well
as scientific laws. Only they must be flexible and
they must be tested. Life is not a rich province to
conquer by our will, or to wring enjoyment out of
with our appetites, nor is it a market where we
pay our money over the counter and receive the
goods we desire. It is rather a great tract of spiritual soil, which we can cultivate or misuse. With
certain restrictions, we have the choice of the
crops which we can grow. Our duty is evidently
to experiment until we find those which grow
most favorably and profitably, to vary our crops
according to the quality of the soil, to protect
them against prowling animals, to keep the ground
clear of noxious weeds. Contending against wind
and weather and pests, we can yet with skill and
vigilance win a living for ourselves. None can
cultivate this garden of our personality but ourselves. Others may supply the seed; it is we who
must plough and reap. We are owners in fee
simple, and we cannot lease. None can live my life
but myself. And the life that I live depends on my
courage, skill, and wisdom in experimentation.

XI

THE DODGING OF PRESSURES

XI

THE DODGING OF PRESSURES

FOR a truly sincere life one talent is needed, —
the ability to steer clear of the forces that would
warp and conventionalize and harden the personality and its own free choices and bents. All the
kingdoms of this world lie waiting to claim the
allegiance of the youth who enters on the career
of life, and sentinels and guards stand ready to
fetter and enslave him the moment he steps un-
warily over the wall out of the free open road of
his own individuality. And unless he dodges them
and keeps straight on his path, dusty and barren
though it may be, he will find himself chained a
prisoner for life, and little by little his own soul
will rot out of him and vanish. The wise men of the
past have often preached the duty of this open
road, they have summoned youth to self-reliance,
but they have not paid sufficient heed to the enemies that would impede his progress. They have
been too intent on encouraging him to be independent and lead his own life, to point out to him
the direction from which the subtle influences that

might control him would come. As a result, young men have too often believed that they were hewing out a career for themselves when they were really simply offering themselves up to some institutional Moloch to be destroyed, or, at the best, passively allowing the career or profession they had adopted to mould and carve them. Instead of working out their own destiny, they were actually allowing an alien destiny to work them out. Youth enters the big world of acting and thinking, a huge bundle of susceptibilities, keenly alive and plastic, and so eager to achieve and perform that it will accept almost the first opportunity that comes to it. Now each youth has his own unique personality and interweaving web of tendencies and inclinations, such as no other person has ever had before. It is essential that these trends and abilities be so stimulated by experience that they shall be developed to their highest capacity. And they can usually be depended upon, if freedom and opportunity are given, to grow of themselves upward towards the sun and air. If a youth does not develop, it is usually because his nature has been blocked and thwarted by the social pressures to which every one of us is subjected, and which only a few have the strength or the wisdom to resist. These pressures come often in the guise of good fortune, and the youth meets them halfway, goes with them gladly, and lets them crush him. He will do it all, too, with so easy a conscience, for is not this meeting the world and making it one's own? It is meeting the world, but it is too often only to have the world make the youth its own.

Our spiritual guides and leaders, then, have been too positive, too heartening, if such a thing be possible. They have either not seen the dangers that lurked in the path, or they have not cared to discourage and depress us by pointing them out. Many of our modern guides, in their panegyrics on success, even glorify as aids on the journey these very dangers themselves, and urge the youth to rely upon them, when he should have been warned not to gaze at all on the dazzling lure. The youth is urged to imitate men who are themselves victims of the very influences that he should dodge, and doctrines and habits are pressed upon him which he should ceaselessly question and never once make his own unless he is sure that they fit him. He will have need to be ever alert to the dangers, and, in early youth at least, would better think more of dodging them than of attaining the goal to which his elders tempt him. Their best service to him would be to warn him against themselves and their influence, rather than to encourage him to become like them.

The dangers that I speak of are the influences and inducements which come to youth from family, business, church, society, state, to compromise with himself and become in more or less degree conformed to their pattern and type. "Be like us!" they all cry, "it is easiest and safest thus! We guarantee you popularity and fortune at so small a price, — only the price of your best self!" Thus they seduce him insidiously rather than openly attack him. They throw their silky chains over him and draw him in. Or they press gently but ceaselessly upon him, rubbing away his original roughness, polishing him down, moulding him relentlessly, and yet with how kindly and solicitous a touch, to their shape and manner. As he feels their caressing pressure against him in the darkness, small wonder is it that he mistakes it for the warm touch of friends and guides. They are friends and guides who always end, however, by being masters and tyrants. They force him to perpetuate old errors, to keep alive dying customs, to breathe new life into vicious prejudices, to take his stand against the saving new. They kill his soul, and then use the carcass as a barricade against the advancing hosts of light. They train him to protect and conserve their own outworn institutions when he should be the first, by reason of his clear insight and freedom from crusted prejudice, to attack them.

The youth's only salvation lies, then, in dodging these pressures. It is not his business to make his own way in life so much as it is to prevent some one else from making it for him. His business is to keep the way clear, and the sky open above his head. Then he will grow and be nurtured according to his needs and his inner nature. He must fight constantly to keep from his head those coverings that institutions and persons in the guise of making him warm and safe throw over his body. If young people would spend half the time in warding away the unfavorable influences that they now spend in conscientiously planning what they are going to be, they would achieve success and maintain their individuality. It seems, curiously enough, that one can live one's true life and guarantee one's individuality best in this indirect way, — not by projecting one's self out upon the world aggressively, but by keeping the

253

track clear along which one's true life may run. A sane, well-rounded, original life is attained not so much by taking thought for it as by the dodging of pressures that would limit and warp its natural growth. The youth must travel the straight road serenely, confident that "his own will come to him." All he must strive for is to recognize his own when it does come, and to absorb and assimilate it. His imagination must be large enough to envisage himself and his own needs. This wisdom, however, comes to too many of us only after we are hopelessly compromised, after we are encrusted over so deeply that, even if we try to break away, our struggles are at the expense of our growth. The first duty of self-conscious youth is to dodge the pressures, his second to survey the world eagerly to see what is "his own." If he goes boldly ahead at first to seek his own, without first making provision for silencing the voices that whisper continually at his side, "Conform!" — he will soon find himself on alien ground, and, if not a prisoner, a naturalized citizen before he has time to think.

Nor is this a mere invitation to whimsicality and eccentricity. These epithets, in our daily life, are somewhat loosely used for all sorts of behavior ranging from nonconformity to pure freakishness. If we really had more original, unspoiled people in the world, we should not use these terms so frequently. If we really had more people who were satisfying their healthy desires, and living the life that their whole inner conscience told them was best, we should not find eccentric or queer the self-sustaining men and women who live without regard to prejudice. And all real whimsicality is a result rather of the thwarting of individuality than of letting it run riot. It is when persons of strong personality are subjected to pressures heavier than they can bear that we get real outbursts of eccentricity. For something unnatural has occurred, a spontaneous flow and progress has been checked. Your eccentric man par excellence is your perfectly conventional man, who never offends in the slightest way by any original action or thought. For he has yielded to every variety of pressure that has been brought to bear upon him, and his original nature has been completely obscured. The pressures have been, however, uniform on every side, so that they have seemingly canceled each other. But this equilibrium simply conceals the forces that have crushed him. The conventional person is, there-

fore, not the most natural but the most unnatural
of persons. His harmlessness is a proof of his
tremendous eccentricity. He has been rubbed
down smooth on all sides like a rock until he has
dropped noiselessly into his place in society. But
at what a cost does he obtain this peace! At the
cost of depersonalizing himself, and sacrificing his
very nature, which, as in every normal person, is
precious and worthy of permanence and growth.
This treason to one's self is perhaps the greatest
mistake of youth, the one unpardonable sin. It is
worse than sowing one's wild oats, for they are
reaped and justice is done; or casting one's bread
upon the waters, for that returneth after many
days. But this sin is the throwing away in willfulness or carelessness the priceless jewel of self-
hood, and with no return, either of recompense or
punishment.

How early and insidious is the pressure upon
us to conform to some type whose fitness we
have not examined, but which we are forced to
take strictly on authority! On the children in the
family what a petty tyranny of ideas and manners
is imposed! Under the guise of being brought
up, how many habits of doubtful value we learned,
how many moral opinions of doubtful significance

we absorbed, how many strange biases that harass and perplex us in our later life we had fastened upon our minds, how many natural and beautiful tendencies we were forced to suppress! The tyranny of manners, of conventional politeness, of puritanical taboos, of superstitious religion, were all imposed upon us for no reason that our elders could devise, but simply that they in turn had had them imposed upon them. Much of our early education was as automatic and unconscious as the handing down of the immemorial traditions in a primitive savage tribe. Now I am far from saying that this household tradition of manners and morals is not an excellent thing for us to acquire. Many of the habits are so useful that it is a wise provision that we should obtain them as naturally as the air we breathe. And it is a pressure that we could not, at that age, avoid, even if we would. But this childhood influence is a sample of true pressure, for it is both unconscious and irresistible. Were we to infringe any of the rules laid down for us, the whole displeasure of the family descended upon our heads; they seemed to vie with each other in expressing their disapproval of our conduct. So, simply to retain our self-respect, we were forced into their pattern of doing things, and for no other reason than that it was their pattern.

This early pressure, however, was mild in comparison with what we experienced as we grew older. We found then that more and more of our actions came insensibly but in some way or other before this court of appeal. We could choose our friends, for instance, only with reservations. If we consorted with little boys who were not clean, or who came from the less reputable portions of the town, we were made to feel the vague family disapproval, perhaps not outspoken, but as an undercurrent to their attitude. And usually we did not need flagrantly to offend to be taught the need of judicious selection, for we were sensitive to the feeling that we knew those around us would entertain, and so avoided the objectionable people from a diffused feeling that they were not "nice." When we grew old enough to move in the youthful social world, we felt this circle of tyranny suddenly widen. It was our "set" now that dictated our choices. The family pressure had been rather subtle and uneasy; this was bold and direct. Here were the most arbitrary selections and disqualifications, girls and boys being banned for no imaginable reason except that they were slightly out of the ordinary, and our little world circumscribed by a rigid public opinion which punished nonconformity by expulsion. If we tried to dodge this pressure and assert our own privileges of making lovers and friends, we were soon delivered an ultimatum, and if we refused to obey, we were speedily cast out into utter darkness, where, strange to say, we lacked even the approbation of the banned. Sometimes we were not allowed to choose our partners to whom we paid our momentary devotions, sometimes we were not allowed to give them up. The price we paid for free participation in the parties and dances and love-affairs of this little social world of youth was an almost military obedience to the general feeling of propriety and suitability of our relationships with others, and to the general will of those in whose circle we went. There was apt to be a rather severe code of propriety, which bore especially upon the girls. Many frank and natural actions and expressions of opinion were thus inhibited, from no real feeling of self-respect, but from the vague, uncomfortable feeling that somebody would not approve. This price for society was one that we were all willing to pay, but it was a bad training. Our own natural likings and dislikings

got blunted; we ceased to seek out our own kind
of people and enjoy them and ourselves in our own
way, but we "went with" the people that our
companions thought we ought to "go with," and
we played the games and behaved generally as
they thought we ought to do.

The family rather corroborated this pressure
than attempted to fortify us in our own individuality. For their honor seemed to be involved
in what we did, and if all our walk in life was
well pleasing to those around us, they were well
pleased with us. And all through life, as long at
least as we were protected under the sheltering
wing of the family, its members constituted a sort
of supreme court over all our relations in life. In
resisting the other pressures that were brought to
bear on us, we rarely found that we had the family's undivided support. They loved, like all social
groups, a smoothly running person, and as soon
as they found us doing unconventional things
or having unusual friends they were vaguely uneasy, as if they were harboring in their midst
some unpredictable animal who would draw upon
them the disapproving glances of the society
around them. The family philosophy has a horror
for the "queer." The table-board is too often a

place where the eccentricities of the world get thoroughly aired. The dread of deviation from accepted standards is impressed upon us from our youth up. The threat which always brought us to terms was, — "If you do this, you will be considered queer!" There was very little fight left in us after that.

But the family has other formidable weapons for bringing us to terms. It knows us through and through as none of our friends and enemies know us. It sees us in undress, when all our outward decorations of spirit and shams and pretenses are thrown off, and it is not deceived by the apologies and excuses that pass muster in the world at large and even to our own conscience. We can conceal nothing from it; it knows all our weakest spots and vulnerable feelings. It does not hesitate to take shameless advantage of that knowledge. Its most powerful weapon is ridicule. It can adopt no subtler method, for we in our turn know all its own vulnerabilities. And where the world at large is generally too polite to employ ridicule upon us, but works with gentler methods of approbation and coldness, our family associates feel no such compunction. Knowing us as they do, they are able to make that ridicule tell. We may have longings for freedom and individuality, but it is a terrible dilemma that faces us. Most men would rather be slaves than butts; they would rather be corralled with the herd than endure its taunts at their independence.

Besides the pressure on a youth or girl to think the way the family does, there is often the pressure brought upon them to sacrifice themselves for its benefit. I do not mean to deprecate that perfectly natural and proper desire to make some return for the care and kindness that have been lavished upon them. But the family insistence often goes much further than this. It demands not only that its young people shall recompense it for what it has done for them, but that they do it in the kind of work and vocation that shall seem proper to it. How often, when the youth or girl is on the point of choosing a congenial occupation or profession, does the family council step in and, with the utmost apparent good-will in the world, dictate differently! And too often the motives are really policy or ambition, or, at best, sheer prejudice. If the youth be not persuaded, then he must bear the brunt of lonely toil without the sympathy or support of those most dear to him. Far harder is the lot of the young woman.

THE DODGING OF PRESSURES

For there is still so much prejudice against a girl's performing useful work in society, apart from her God-given duty of getting married, that her initiative is crushed at the very beginning. The need of cultivating some particular talent or interest, even if she has not to earn her living, seems to be seldom felt. Yet women, with their narrower life, have a greater need of sane and vigorous spiritual habits than do men. It is imperative that a girl be prevented from growing up into a useless, fleshly, and trivial woman, of the type one sees so much of nowadays. Even if a girl does marry, a few intellectual interests and gifts and tastes will not be found to detract from her charm or usefulness. The world never needed so much as it does to-day women of large hearts and large minds, whose home and sphere are capable of embracing something beyond the four corners of their kitchen. And the world can get such women only by allowing them the initiative and opportunity to acquire varied interests and qualities while they are young.

The family often forges sentimental bonds to keep it living together long after the motive and desire have departed. There is no group so uncongenial as an uncongenial family. The constant rubbing together accentuates all the divergencies and misunderstandings. Yet sometimes a family whose members are hopelessly mismated will cling together through sheer inertia or through a conscientious feeling of duty. And duty to too many of us is simply a stimulus to that curious love for futile suffering that form sone of the darker qualities of the puritan soul. Family duty may not only warp and mutilate many a life that would bloom healthily outside in another environment, but it may actually mean the pauperization of the weaker members. The claims of members of the family upon each other are often overwhelming, and still more often quite fictitious in their justice. Yet that old feeling of the indissolubility of the family will often allow the weak, who might, if forced to shift for themselves, become strong, to suck the lifeblood from the stronger members. Coöperation, when it is free and spontaneous and on a basis of congeniality, is the foundation of all social life and progress, but forced cohesion can do little good. The average family is about as well mated as any similar group would be, picked out at random from society. And this means, where the superstition of indissolubility is still effective, that the members share not only all the benefits, but also all each others' shortcomings and irritations. Family life thus not only presses upon its youth to conform to its customs and habits and to the opinions of the little social world in which it lives, but also drags its youth down with its claims, and warps it by its tension of uncongeniality, checks its spontaneity by its lack of appreciation, and injures its soul by friction and misunderstanding.

This family pressure upon youth is serious, and potent for much good and evil in his later life. It is necessary that he understand how to analyze it without passion or prejudice, and find out just how he can dodge the unfavorable pressure without injury to the love that is borne him or the love that he bears to the others. But let him not believe that his love is best shown by submission. It is best shown by a resolute determination and assertion of his own individuality. Only he must know, without the cavil of a doubt, what that individuality is; he must have a real imaginative anticipation of its potentialities. Only with this intuition will he know where to dodge and how to dodge.

It is true that the modern generation seems to be changing all this. Family cohesion and authority no longer mean what they did even twenty years ago. The youth of to-day are willful, selfish, heartless, in their rebellion. They are changing the system blindly and blunderingly. They feel the pressure, and without stopping to ask questions or analyze the situation, they burst the doors and flee away. Their seeming initiative is more animal spirits than anything else. They have exploded the myth that their elders have any superhuman wisdom of experience to share with them, or any incontrovertible philosophy of life with which to guide their wandering footsteps. But it must be admitted that most have failed so far to find a wisdom and a philosophy to take its place. They have too often thrown away the benefits of family influence on account of mere trivialities of misunderstanding. They have not waited for the real warpings of initiative, the real pressure of prejudice, but have kicked up their heels at the first breath of authority. They have not so much dodged the pressure as fled it altogether. Instead of being intent on brushing away the annoying obstacles that interfered with the free growth of their own worthier selves, they have mistaken the means for the end, and have merely brushed off the interferences, without first having any consciousness of that worthier self. Now of course this is no solution. It is only as they substitute for the authority that they throw off a definite authority of their own, crystallized out of their own ideals and purposes, that they will gain or help others to gain. For lack of a vision the people perish. For lack of a vision of their own personalities, and the fresh, free, aggressive, forward, fearless, radical life that we all ought to lead, and could lead if we only had the imagination for it, the youth of to-day will cast off the narrowing confining fetters of authority only to wander without any light at all. This is not to say that this aimless wandering is not better than the prison-house, but it is to say that the emancipation of the spirit is insufficient without a new means of spiritual livelihood to take its place. The youth of to-day cannot rest on their liberation; they must see their freedom as simply the setting free of forces within themselves for a cleaner, sincerer life, and for radical work in society. The road is cut out before them by pioneers; they have but to let themselves grow out in that direction.

I have painted the family pressures in this somewhat lurid hue because they are patterns of the other attacks which are made upon the youth as he meets the world. The family is a little microcosm, a sheltered group where youth feels all those currents of influence that sway men in their social life. Some of them are exaggerated, some perverted, but they are most of them there in that little world. It is no new discovery that in family life one can find heaven or one can find hell. The only pressure that is practically absent in the family is the economic pressure, by which I mean the inducements, and even necessities, that a youth is under of conforming to codes or customs and changing his ideals and ideas, when he comes to earn his livelihood. This pressure affects him as soon as he looks for an opening, as he calls it, in which to make his living. At that time all this talk of natural talents or bents or interests begin to sound far-away and ideal. He soon finds that these things have no commercial value in themselves and will go but a short way towards providing him with his living. The majority of us "go to work" as soon as our short "education" is completed, if not before, and we go not by choice, but wherever opportunity is given. Hence the ridiculous misfits, the apathy, the restlessness and discontent. The world of young people around us seems too largely to be one where both men and girls are engaged in work in which they have no interest, and for which they have no aptitude. They are mournfully fettered to their work; all they can seem to do is to make the best of it, and snatch out of the free moments what pleasure and exhilaration they can. They have little hope for a change. There is too much of a scramble for places in this busy, crowded world, to make a change anything but hazardous. It is true that restlessness often forces a change, but it is rarely for the better, or in the line of any natural choice or interest. One leaves one's job, but then one takes thankfully the first job that presents itself; the last state may be worse than the first. By this economic pressure most of us are sidetracked, turned off from our natural path, and fastened irrevocably to some work that we could only acquire an interest in at the expense of our souls.

It is a pressure, too, that cannot easily be dodged. We can frankly recognize our defeat, plunge boldly at the work and make it a part of ourselves; this course of action, which most of us adopt, is really, however, simply an unconditional surrender. We can drift along apathetically, without interest either in our work or our own personalities; this course is even more disastrous. Or we can quietly wait until we have found the vocation that guarantees the success of our personalities; this course is an ideal that is possible to very few. And yet, did we but know it, a little thought at the beginning would often have prevented the misfit, and a little boldness when one has discovered the misfit would often have secured the favorable change. That self-recognition, which is the only basis for a genuine spiritual success in life, is the thing that too many of us lack. The apathy comes from a real ignorance of what our true work is. Then we are twice a slave, — a prey to our circumstance and a prey to our ignorance.

Like all discoveries, what one's work is can be found only by experiment. But this can often be an imaginative experiment. One can take an "inventory of one's personality," and discover one's interests, and the kind of activity one feels at home with or takes joy in. Yet it is true that there are many qualities which cannot be discovered by the imagination, which need the fairy touch of actual use to develop them. There is no royal road to this success. Here the obstacles are usually too thick to be dodged. We do not often enough recognize the incredible stupidity of our civilization where so much of the work is uninteresting and monotonous. That we should consider it a sort of triumph that a man like Mr. John Burroughs should have been able to live his life as he chose, travel along his own highroad, and develop himself in his own natural direction, is a curious reflection on our ideals of success and on the incompleteness of our civilization. Such a man has triumphed, however, because he has known what to dodge. He has not been crushed by the social opinion of his little world, or lured by specious success, or fettered by his "job," or hoodwinked by prejudice. He has kept his spirit clear and pure straight through life. It would be well for modern youth if it could let an ideal like this color their lives, and permeate all their thoughts and ambitions. It would be well if they could keep before them such an ideal as a pillar of fire by day and a cloud by night.

If we cannot dodge this economic pressure, at least we can face it. If we are situated so that we have no choice in regard to our work, we may still resist the influences which its uncongeniality would bring to bear upon us. This is not done by forcing an interest in it, or liking for it. If the work is socially wasteful or useless or even pernicious, as so much business and industrial work to-day is, it is our bounden duty not to be interested in it or to like it. We should not be playing our right place in society if we enjoyed such a prostitution of energies. One of the most insidious of the economic pressures is this awaking the interest of youth in useless and wasteful work, work that takes away energy from production to dissipate in barter and speculation and all the thousand ways that men have discovered of causing money to flow from one pocket to another without the transference of any fair equivalent of real wealth. We can dodge these pressures not by immolating ourselves, but by letting the routine work lie very lightly on our soul. We can understand clearly the nature and effects of this useless work we are doing, and keep it from either alluring or smothering us. We can cultivate a disinterested aloofness towards it, and keep from breathing its poisonous atmosphere. The extra hours we can fill with real interests, and make them glow with an intensity that will make our life almost as rich as if we were wholly given over to a real lifework. We can thus live in two worlds, one of which is the more precious because it is one of freedom from very real oppression. And that oppression will seem light because it has the réverse shield of liberty. If we do drudgery, it must be our care to see that it does not stifle us. The one thing needful in all our work and play is that we should always be on top, that our true personality should always be in control. Our life must not be passive, running simply by the momentum furnished by another; it must have the motive power within itself; although it gets the fuel from the stimulation of the world about it, the steam and power must be manufactured within itself.

These counsels of aloofness from drudgery suggest the possibilities of avoiding the economic pressures where they are too heavy completely to dodge, and where the work is an irrevocable misfit. But the pressures of success are even more deadly than those of routine. How early is one affected by that first pressure of worldly opinion which says that lack of success in business or a profession is disgraceful! The one devil of our modern world is failure, and many are the charms used by the medicine men to ward him away. If we lived in a state of society where virtue was its own reward, where our actions were automatically measured and our rewards duly proportioned to our efforts, a lack of success would be a real indication of weakness and flaw, or, at best, ill-preparation. But where business success is largely dependent on the possession of capital, a lucky risk, the ability to intimidate or deceive, and where professional success is so often dependent upon self-assertion or some irrelevant but pleasing trait of personality, failure means nothing more than bad luck, or, at most, inability to please those clients to whom one has made one's appeal. To dodge this pressure of fancied failure and humiliation is to have gone a long way towards guaranteeing one's real success.. We are justified in adopting a pharisaical attitude towards success, — "Lord, I thank thee that I have not succeeded as other men have!" To have judged one's self by the inner standards of truth to one's own personality, to count the consciousness of having done well, regardless of the corroboration of a public, as success, is to have avoided this most discouraging of pressures.

It is even doubtful whether business or professional success, except in the domain of science and art, can be attained without a certain betrayal of soul. The betrayal may have been small, but at some point one has been compressed, one has yielded to alien forces and conformed to what the heart did not give assent to. It may be that one has kept silent when one should have spoken, that one has feigned interests and enthusiasms, or done work that one knew was idle and useless, in order to achieve some goal; but always that goal has been reached not spontaneously but under a foreign pressure. More often than not the fortunate one has not felt the direct pressure, has not been quite conscious of the sacrifice, but only vaguely uneasy and aware that all was not right within him, and has won his peace only by drugging his uneasiness with visions of the final triumph. The pressure is always upon him to keep silent and conform. He must not only adopt all the outward forms and ceremonies, as in the family and social life, but he must also adopt the traditional ideals.

The novice soon finds that he is expected to defend the citadel, even against his own heresies. The lawyer who finds anomalies in the law, injustice in the courts, is not encouraged to publish abroad his facts, or make proposals for reform. The student who finds antiquated method, erroneous hypotheses in his subject, is not expected to use his knowledge and his genius to remodel the study. The minister who comes upon·new and living interpretations for his old creeds is not encouraged to speak forth the truth that is in him. Nor is the business man who finds corrupt practices in his business encouraged to give the secrets away. There is a constant social pressure on these "reformers" to leave things alone.

And this does not arise from any corrupt connivance with the wrong, or from any sympathy with the evildoers. The cry rises equally from the corrupt and the holy, from the men who are responsible for the abuses and those who are innocent, from those who know of them and those who do not. It is simply the instinctive reaction of the herd against anything that savors of the unusual; it is the tendency of every social group simply to resist change. This alarm at innovation is universal, from college presidents to Catholic peasants, in fashionable club or sewing circle or political party. On the radical there is immediately brought, without examination, without reason or excuse, the whole pressure of the organization to stultify his vision and force him back into the required grooves. The methods employed are many: a warning is issued against him as being unsound and unsafe; his motive is to make trouble, or revenge himself on the directors for some slight; finally he is solemnly pilloried as an "enemy of the people." Excellent reasons are discovered for his suppression. Effective working of an organization requires coöperation, but also subordination; in the interests of efficiency, therefore, individual opinion cannot be allowed full sway. The reputation of the organization before the world depends on its presenting a harmonious and united front; internal disagreements and criticisms tend to destroy the respect of the public. Smoothness of working is imperative; a certain individual liberty must, therefore, be sacrificed for the success of the organization. And if these plausible excuses fail, there is always the appeal to authority and to tried and tested experience. Now all these reasons are simply apologies brought up after the fact to justify the first instinctive reaction. What they all mean is this, and only this: He would unsettle things; away with him!

In olden times, they had sterner ways of enforcing these pressures. But although the stake and dungeon have disappeared, the spirit of con-

servatism does not seem to have changed very
much. Educated men still defend the hoariest
abuses, still stand sponsor for utterly antiquated
laws and ideals. That is why the youth of this
generation has to be so suspicious of those who
seem to speak authoritatively. He knows not
whom he can trust, for few there are who speak
from their own inner conviction. Most of our
leaders and moulders of public opinion speak
simply as puppets pulled by the strings of the
conservative bigotry of their class or group. It is
well that the youth of to-day should know this,
for the knowledge will go far towards steeling
him against that most insidious form of pressure
that comes from the intellectual and spiritual
prestige of successful and honored men. When
youth sees that a large part of their success has
been simply their succumbing to social pressure,
and that their honor is based largely on the fact
that they do not annoy vested interests with proposals or agitations for betterment, he will seek to
discover new standards of success, and find his
prophets and guides among the less fortunate,
perhaps, but among those who have retained their
real integrity. This numbing palsy of conservative assent which steals over so many brilliant

and sincere young men as they are subjected to the influence of prestige and authority in their profession is the most dangerous disease that threatens youth. It can be resisted only by constant criticism and candid vigilance. "Prove all things; hold fast to that which is good," should be the motto of the intellectual life. Only by testing and comparing all the ideals that are presented to one is it possible to dodge that pressure of authority that would crush the soul's original enthusiasms and beliefs. Not doubt but convention is the real enemy of youth.

Yet these spiritual pressures are comparatively easy to dodge when one is once awake to them. It is the physical pressure that those in power are able to bring to bear upon the dissenter that constitutes the real problem. The weak man soon becomes convinced of his hardihood and audacity in supposing that his ideas could be more valuable than the running tradition, and recants his heresies. But those who stick stiff-neckedly out are soon crushed. When the youth is settled in life, has trained for his profession and burned his bridges behind him, it means a great deal to combat authority. For those in power can make use of the economic pressure to force him to conformity. It is the shame of our universities that they are giving constant illustrations of this use of arbitrary power, directed usually against nonconformity in social and political opinion. Recent examples show the length to which even these supposedly enlightened institutions are willing to go to prevent social heresy in their midst. Often such harsh measures are not needed. A subtle appeal to a man's honor is effective. "While you are a member of a society," it is said, "it is your duty to think in harmony with its ideals and policies. If you no longer agree with those ideals, it is your duty to withdraw. You can fight honorably for your own ideas only from the outside." All that need be said about this doctrine, so fair and reasonable on the surface, is that it contains all the philosophic support that would perpetuate the evil of the world forever. For it means attacking vested evil from the weakest vantage-point; it means willfully withdrawing to the greatest distance, shooting one's puny arrows at the citadel, and then expecting to capture it. It means also to deny any possibility of progress within the organization itself. For as soon as dissent from the common inertia developed, it would be automatically eliminated. It is a principle, of course, that plays directly into the hands of the conservators. It is an appeal to honor that is dishonorable. Let it seduce no man's sincerity!

The principal object of every organization, as every youth soon discovers who feels dissatisfaction with the policies of church, club, college, or party, is to remain true to type. Each is organized with a central vigilance committee, whose ostensible function is direction, but whose real business is to resist threatening change and keep matters as they are. The ideal is smoothness; every part of the machine is expected to run along in its well-oiled groove. Youths who have tried to introduce their new ideas into such organizations know the weight of this fearful resistance. It seems usually as if all the wisdom and experience of these elders had taught them only the excellence of doing nothing at all. Their favorite epithet for those who have individual opinions is "troublemakers," forgetting that men do not run the risk of the unpopularity and opprobrium that aggressiveness always causes, for the sheer love of making trouble. Through an instinct of self-preservation, such an organization always places loyalty above truth, the permanence of the organization above the permanence of its principles. Even in

281

churches we are told that to alter one's opinion of a creed to which one has once given allegiance is basely to betray one's higher nature. These are the pressures that keep wavering men in the footpaths where they have once put their feet, and stunts their truer, growing selves. How many souls a false loyalty has blunted none can say; perhaps almost as many as false duty!

In the dodging of these pressures many a man finds the real spiritual battle of his life. They are a challenge to all his courage and faith. Unless he understands their nature, his defeat will bring despair or cynicism. When the group is weak and he is strong, he may resist successfully, press back in his turn, actually create a public opinion that will support him, and transfuse it all with his new spirit and attitude. Fortunate, indeed, is he who can not only dodge these pressures but dissolve them! If he is weak and his efforts are useless, and the pressure threatens to crush him, he would better withdraw and let the organization go to its own diseased perdition. If he can remain within without sacrifice to his principles, this is well, for then he has a vantage-ground for the enunciation of those principles. Eternal vigilance, however, is the price of his liberty.

THE DODGING OF PRESSURES

The secret ambition of the group seems to be to turn out all its members as nearly alike as possible. It seeks to create a type to which all new adherents shall be moulded. Each group, then, that we have relations with is ceaselessly working to mould us to its type and pattern. It is this marvellous unseen power that a group has of forming after its own image all that come under its influence, that conquers men. It has the two instincts of self-preservation and propagation strongly developed, and we tend unthinkingly to measure its value in terms of its success in the expression of those instincts. Rather should it be measured always in terms of its ability to create and stimulate varied individuality. This is the new ideal of social life. This is what makes it so imperative that young men of to-day should recognize and dodge the pressures that would thwart the assertion of this ideal. The aim of the group must be to cultivate personality, leaving open the road for each to follow his own. The bond of cohesion will be the common direction in which those roads point, but this is far from saying that all the travelers must be alike. It is enough that there be a common aim and a common ideal.

Societies are rarely content with this, however; they demand a close mechanical similarity, and a conformity to a reactionary and not a progressive type. If we would be resolute in turning our gaze towards the common aim, and dodging the pressure of the common pattern, our family, business, and social life would be filled with a new spirit. We can scarcely imagine the achievement and liberation that would result. Individuality would come to its own; it would no longer be suspect. Youth would no longer be fettered and bound, but would come to its own as the leaven and even leader of life. Men would worship progress as they now worship stagnation; their ideal in working together would be a living effectiveness instead of a mechanical efficiency.

This gospel is no call to ease and comfort. It is rather one of peril. The youth of this generation will not be so lightly seduced, or go so innocently into the bonds of conservatism and convention, under the impression that they are following the inspired road to success. Their consciences will be more delicate. They know now the dangers that confront them and the road they are called on to tread. It is not an easy road. It is beset with opportunities for real eccentricity, for

284

selfishness, for willfulness, for mere bravado. It would be surprising, after the long premium that has been placed on the pattern, not to see a reaction in favor of sheer freakishness. Many of our modern radicals are examples of this reaction. Yet their method is so sound, their goal so clear and noble, their spirit so sincere, that they are true pioneers of the new individuality. Their raciness is but the raciness of all pioneers everywhere. And much of their irresponsibility is a result of that intolerable pressure against which they are revolting. They have dodged it, but it dogs them and concentrates itself sullenly behind them to punish them for their temerity. The scorn of the world hurts and hampers them. That ridicule which the family employed against deviation is employed in all large social movements against the innovators. Yet slowly and surely the new social ideal makes its way.

It is not a call to the surrendering of obligations, in family or business or profession, but it is a call to the criticism of obligations. Youth must distinguish carefully between the essential duties and the non-essential, between those which make for the realization of the best common ideals, and those which make merely for the maintenance of a dogma or unchallenged superstition. By resisting the pressures that would warp, do we really best serve society; by allowing our free personality to develop, do we contribute most to the common good. We must recognize that our real duty is always found running in the direction of our worthiest desires. No duty that runs rough-shod over the personality can have a legitimate claim upon us. We serve by being as well as by doing.

It is easy to distort this teaching into a counsel to unbridled selfishness. And that, of course, is the risk. But shall we not dare to take the risk? It may be also that in our care to dodge the pressures, we may lose all the inestimable influences of good that come along mixed in with the hurtful. But shall we not take the risk? Our judgments can only grow by exercise; we can only learn by constantly discriminating. Self-recognition is necessary to know one's road, but, knowing the road, the price of the mistakes and perils is worth paying. The following of that road will be all the discipline one needs. Discipline does not mean being moulded by outside forces, but sticking to one's road against the forces that would deflect or bury the soul. People speak of finding one's niche in the world. Society, as we have seen, is

THE DODGING OF PRESSURES

one vast conspiracy for carving one into the kind of a statue it likes, and then placing it in the most convenient niche it has. But for us, not the niche but the open road, with the spirit always traveling, always criticizing, always learning, always escaping the pressures that threaten its integrity. With its own fresh power it will keep strong and true to the journey's end.

XII

FOR RADICALS

XII

FOR RADICALS

THE great social movement of yesterday and to-day and to-morrow has hit us of the younger generation hard. Many of us were early converted to a belief in the possibilities of a regenerated social order, and to a passionate desire to do something in aid of that regeneration. The appeal is not only to our sympathy for the weak and exploited, but also to our delight in a healthy, free, social life, to an artistic longing for a society where the treasures of civilization may be open to all, and to our desire for an environment where we ourselves will be able to exercise our capacities, and exert the untrammeled influences which we believe might be ours and our fellows'. All these good things the social movement seems to demand and seems to offer, and its appeal is irresistible. Before the age of machinery was developed, or before the structure of our social system and the relations between classes and individuals was revealed, the appeal might have been merely sentimental. But it is no longer so. The aims of the social movement to-day seem to have all the tremendous power of a practicable ideal. To the satisfactions which its separate ideals give to all the finer instincts of men is added the overwhelming conviction that those satisfactions are most of them realizable here and now by concerted methods which are already partly in operation and partially successful. It is this union of the idealistic and the efficient that gives the movement its hold on the disinterested and serious youth of to-day.

With that conversion has necessarily come the transvaluation of many of our social values. No longer can we pay the conventional respect to success or join in the common opinions of men and causes. The mighty have been pulled down from their seats, and those of low degree exalted. We feel only contempt for college presidents, editors, and statesmen who stultify their talents and pervert their logical and historical knowledge in defending outworn political philosophies and economic codes. We can no longer wholly believe in the usefulness or significance of those teachers and writers who show themselves serenely oblivious to the social problems. We become keen analysts of the society around us; we put uncomfortable questions to our sleek and successful elders. We criticize the activities in which they engage, the hitherto sacred professions and businesses, and learn to distinguish carefully between actually productive work for society, work which makes for the material and spiritual well-being of the people for whom it is done, and parasitic or wasteful work, which simply extends the friction of competition, or lives on the labor or profits of others. We distinguish, too, between the instruction and writing that consists in handing down unexamined and uncriticized moral and political ideas, and ideas that let in the fresh air and sunlight to the thick prejudices of men. We come to test the papers we read, the teachers we learn from, the professional men we come into contact with, by these new standards. Various and surprising are the new interweavings we discover, and the contrasts and ironies of the modern intellectual life. The childlike innocence in which so many seem still to slumber is almost incredible to those whose vision is so clear. The mechanical way in which educated men tend to absorb and repeat whole systems of formulas is a constant surprise to those whose ideas hum and clash and react against each other. But the minds of so many of these men of position seem to run in automatic channels, such that, given one set of opinions, one could predict with accuracy their whole philosophy of life. Our distrust of their whole spiritual fabric thus becomes fundamental. We can no longer take most of them seriously. It is true that they are doing the serious work of the world, while we do nothing as yet except criticize, and perhaps are doomed to fail altogether when we try. To be sure, it is exactly their way of doing that serious work that we object to, but still we are the dreamers, they the doers; we are the theorists, they the practical achievers. Yet the precision of our view will not down; we can see in their boasted activity little but a resolute sitting on the lid, a sort of glorified routine of keeping the desk clear. And we would rather remain dreamers, we feel, than do much of their work. Other values we find are changed. We become hopelessly perverted by democracy. We no longer make the careful distinctions between the fit and the unfit, the successful and the unsuccessful, the effective and the ineffective, the presentable and the unpresentable. We are more interested in the influences that have produced these seeming differences than in the fact of the differences themselves. We classify people by new categories. We look for personality, for sincerity, for social sympathy, for democratic feeling, for social productiveness, and we interpret success in terms of these attainments.

The young radical, then, in such a situation and in possession of these new social values, stands on the verge of his career in a mood of great perplexity. Two questions he must answer, — "What is to be done?" and "What must I do?" If he has had an education and is given a real opportunity for the choice of a vocation, his position is crucial. For his education, if it has been in one of the advanced universities, will have only tended to confirm his radicalism and render more vivid the contrast between the new philosophy which is being crystallized there out of modern science and philosophy and the new interpretations of history and ethics, and the obscurantist attitude of so many of our intellectual guardians. The youth, ambitious and aggressive, desires an effective and serviceable career, yet every career open to him seems a compromise with the old order. If he has come to see the law as an attempt to fit immutable principles of social action on a dynamic and ever-growing society; if he has come to see the church as an organization working along the lines of greatest spiritual resistance, preaching a personal where the world is crying for a social gospel; if he has come to see higher education as an esoteric institution of savants, only casually reaching down to touch the mass of people with their knowledge and ideas; if he has come to see business as a clever way of distributing unearned wealth, and the levying of a refined tribute on the propertyless workers; if he has come to see the press as devoted to bolstering up all these institutions in their inefficiency and inertia; — if he has caught this radical vision of the social institutions about him, he will find it hard to fit neatly into any of them and let it set its brand upon him. It would seem to be a treason not only to society but to his own best self. He would seem to have become one of the vast conspiracy to keep things as they are. He has spent his youth, perhaps, in studying things as they are in order to help in changing them into things as they ought to be, but he is now confronted with the question how the change can be accomplished, and how he can help in that accomplishment.

The attempt to answer these questions seems at first to bring him to a deadlock and to inhibit all his powers. He desires self-development and self-expression, and the only opportunities offered him seem to be ways of life and training that will only mock the best social ideals that he has. This is the dilemma of latter-day youth, and it is a dilemma which is new and original to our own age. Earnest men and women have always had before them the task of adjusting themselves to this world, of "overcoming the world," but the proper method has always been found in withdrawing from it altogether, or in passing through it with as little spot and blemish as possible, not in plunging into its activity and attempting to subjugate it to one's ideals. Yet this is the task that the young radical sets for himself. Subjugation without compromise! But so many young men and women feel that this is impossible. Confident of their sincerity, yet distrustful of their strength, eager yet timorous, they stand on the brink, longing to serve, but not knowing how, and too likely, through their distrust and fears, to make a wreck of their whole lives. They feel somehow that they have no right to seek their own welfare or the training of their own talents until they have paid that service to society which they have learned is its due.

It does not do to tell them that one of their best services will be that training. They demand some more direct way of influencing their fellows, some short road to radical activity. It would be good for them to know that they cannot hope to accomplish very much in radiating their ideals without the skill and personality which gives impetus to that radiation. Good-will alone has little efficacy. For centuries well-wishers of men have shown a touching faith in the power of pure ideals to propagate themselves. The tragic failures of the beginnings of the social movement itself were largely due to this belief. Great efforts ended only in sentimentality. But we have no intention now that the fund of intellectual and spiritual energy liberated by radical thought in the younger generation shall die away in such ineffective efforts. To radiate influence, one's light must shine before men, and it must glow, moreover, with a steady and resolute flame, or men will neither see nor believe the good works that are being done.

It would be an easy way out of the dilemma if we could all adopt the solution of Kropotkin, the Russian radical writer, and engage in radical journalism. This seems to be the most direct

means of bringing one's ideals to the people, to be
a real fighting on the firing line. It is well to
remember, however, that a weak propagandist
is a hindrance rather than an assistance, and that
the social movement needs the best of talent, and
the skill. This is a challenge to genius, but it is
also a reminder that those who fight in other ranks
than the front may do as valiant and worthy service. One of the first lessons the young radical
has to learn is that influence can be indirect as
well as direct, and will be strongest when backed
by the most glowing personality. So that self-
cultivation becomes almost a duty, if one wants to
be effective towards the great end. And not only
personality but prestige; for the prestige of the
person from whom ideals come is one of the strongest factors in driving home those ideas to the
mind of the hearer and making them a motive
force in his life. Vested interests do not hesitate
to make use of the services of college presidents
and other men of intellectual prestige to give their
practices a philosophic support; neither should
radicals disdain, as many seem to disdain, the use
of prestige as a vantage-ground from which to
hurl their dogmas. Even though Kropotkin himself deprecated his useless learning, his scientific

reputation has been a great factor in spreading his radical ideas.

It is the fashion among some radicals to despise the applause of the conventional, unthinking mass, and scorn any success which has that appreciation as an ingredient. But this is not the way to influence that same crass, unthinking mass or convert it to one's doctrines. It is to alienate at the beginning the heathen to whom the gospel is being brought. And even the radical has the right to be wise as a serpent and harmless as a dove. He must see merely that his distinctiveness is based on real merit and not, as many reputations are, on conformity to an established code. Scientific research, engineering, medicine, and any honest craft, are vocations where it is hard to win prestige without being socially productive; their only disadvantage lies in the fact that their activity does not give opportunity for the influence of the kind the radical wishes to exert. Art, literature, and teaching are perilous; the pressures to conform are deadly, but the triumphs of individuality splendid. For one's daily work lies there directly in the line of impressing other minds. The genius can almost swing the lash over men's spirits, and form their ideas for them; he combines enormous prestige with enormous direct influence. Law, the ministry, and business seem to be peculiarly deadly; it is hard to see how eminence can be attained in those professions except at the cost of many of one's social ideals.

The radical can thus choose his career with full knowledge of the social possibilities. Where he is forced by economic necessity to engage in distasteful and unsocial work, he may still leave no doubt, in the small realm he does illuminate, as to his attitude and his purpose, his enthusiasm and his hope. For all his powers and talents can be found to contribute something; fusing together they form his personality and create his prestige, and it is these that give the real impetus and the vital impulse that drive one's beliefs and ideals into the hearts of other men. If he speaks, he will be listened to, for it is faith and not doubt that men strain their ears to hear. It is the believing word that they are eager to hear. Let the social faith be in a youth, and it will leak out in every activity of his life, it will permeate his words and color his deeds. The belief and the vision are the essentials; these given, there is little need for him to worry how he may count in society. He will count in spite of himself. He may never know just how he is counting, he may never hear the reverberations of his own personality in others, but reverberate it will, and the timbre and resonance will be in proportion to the quality and power of that vision.

The first concrete duty of every youth to whom social idealism is more than a phrase is to see that he is giving back to society as much as or more than he receives, and, moreover, that he is a nourisher of the common life and not a drain upon its resources. This was Tolstoy's problem, and his solution to the question — "What is to be done?" — was — "Get off the other fellow's back!" His duty, he found, was to arrange his life so that the satisfaction of his needs did not involve the servitude or the servility of any of his fellow men; to do away with personal servants, and with the articles of useless luxury whose production meant the labor of thousands who might otherwise have been engaged in some productive and life-bringing work; to make his own living either directly from the soil, or by the coöperative exchange of services, in professional, intellectual, artistic, or handicraft labor. Splendidly sound as this solution is, both ethically and economically, the tragic fact remains that so inextricably are we woven into the social web that we cannot live except in some degree at the expense of somebody else, and that somebody is too often a man, woman, or even little child who gives grudgingly, painfully, a stint of labor that we may enjoy. We do not see the labor and the pain, and with easy hearts and quiet consciences we enjoy what we can of the good things of life; or, if we see the truth, as Tolstoy saw it, we still fancy, like him, that we have it in our power to escape the curse by simple living and our own labor. But the very food we eat, the clothes we wear, the simplest necessities of life with which we provide ourselves, have their roots somewhere, somehow, in exploitation and injustice. It is a cardinal necessity of the social system under which we live that this should be so, where the bulk of the work of the world is done, not for human use and happiness, but primarily and directly for the profits of masters and owners. We are all tainted with the original sin; we cannot escape our guilt. And we can be saved out of it only by the skill and enthusiasm which we show in our efforts to change things. We cannot help the poisonous soil from which our sustenance springs, but we can be laboring mightily at agitating that soil, ploughing it, turning it, and sweetening it, against the day when new seed will be planted and a fairer fruitage be produced.

The solution of these dilemmas of radical youth will, therefore, not come from a renunciation of the personality or a refusal to participate actively in life. Granted the indignation at our world as it is, and the vision of the world as it might and ought to be, both the heightening of all the powers of the personality and a firm grappling with some definite work-activity of life are necessary to make that indignation powerful and purging, and to transmute that vision into actual satisfaction for our own souls and those of our fellows. It is a fallacy of radical youth to demand all or nothing, and to view every partial activity as compromise. Either engage in something that will bring revolution and transformation all at one blow, or do nothing, it seems to say. But compromise is really only a desperate attempt to reconcile the irreconcilable. It is not compromise to study to understand the world in which one lives, to seek expression for one's inner life, to work to harmonize it and make it an integer, nor is it compromise to work in some small sphere for the harmonization of social life and the relations between men who work together, a harmonization that will bring democracy into every sphere of life, industrial and social.

Radical youth is apt to long for some supreme sacrifice and feels that a lesser surrender is worth nothing. But better than sacrifice is efficiency! It is absurd to stand perplexedly waiting for the great occasion, unwilling to make the little efforts and test the little occasions, and unwilling to work at developing the power that would make those occasions great. Of all the roads of activity that lie before the youth at the threshold of life, one paramount road must be taken. This fear that one sees so often in young people, that, if they choose one of their talents or interests or opportunities of influence and make themselves in it "competent ones of their generation," they must slaughter all the others, is irrational. It is true that the stern present demands singleness of purpose and attention. A worthy success is impossible to-day if the labor is divided among many interests. In a more leisurely time, the soul could encompass many fields, and even to-day the genius may conquer and hold at once many spiritual kingdoms. But this is simply a stern challenge to us all to make ourselves geniuses. For serious and sincere as the desire of radical youth may

305

be to lead the many-sided life, a life without a
permanent core of active and productive interest,
of efficient work in the world, leads to dilettant-
ism and triviality. Such efficient work, instead of
killing the other interests of life, rather fertilizes
them and makes them in turn enrich the central
activity. Instead of feeding on their time, it
actually creates time for the play of the other
interests, which is all the sweeter for its preciousness.

Always trying to make sure that the work, apart
from the inevitable taint of exploitation which is
involved in modern work, is socially productive,
that it actually in some way contributes to the
material or spiritual welfare of the people for
whom it is done, and does not simply reiterate
old formulas, does not simply extend the friction
of competition or consist simply in living on the
labor and profits of others. Such work cannot be
found by rule. The situation is a real dilemma for
the idealistic youth of to-day, and its solution is
to be worked out in the years to come. It is these
crucial dilemmas that make this age so difficult
to live in, that make life so hard to harmonize and
integrate. The shock of the crassnesses and crud-
ities of the modern social world thrown against

the conventionally satisfying picture which that
world has formed of itself makes any young life of
purpose and sincerity a real peril and adventure.
There are all sorts of spiritual disasters lying in
wait for the youth who embarks on the perilous
ocean of radicalism. The disapproval of those
around him is likely to be the least of his dangers. It should rather fortify his soul than discourage him. Far more dangerous is it that he
lose his way on the uncharted seas before him, or
follow false guides to shipwreck. But the solution
is not to stay at home, fearful and depressed. It is
rather to cultivate deliberately the widest knowledge, the broadest sympathy, the keenest insight,
the most superb skill, and then set sail, exulting
in one's resources, and crowding on every inch
of sail.

For if the radical life has its perils, it also has its
great rewards. The strength and beauty of the
radical's position is that he already to a large
extent lives in that sort of world which he desires.
Many people there are who would like to live in
a world arranged in some sort of harmony with
socialistic ideals, but who, believing they are
impossible, dismiss the whole movement as an idle
if delightful dream. They thus throw away all the

opportunity to have a share in the extending of those ideals. They do not see that the gradual infiltration of those ideals into our world as it is does brighten and sweeten it enormously. They do not know the power and advantage of even their "little faith" which their inclinations might give them. But the faith of the radical has already transformed the world in which he lives. He sees the "muddle" around him, but what he actually feels and lives are the germs of the future. His mind selects out the living, growing ideas and activities of the socially fruitful that exist here and now, and it is with these that his soul keeps company; it is to their growth and cultivation that he is responsive. This is no illusion that he knows, no living in a pleasing but futile world of fancy. For this living the socialistic life as far as he is able, he believes has its efficient part in creating that communal life of the future. He feels himself, not as an idle spectator of evolution, but as an actual co-worker in the process. He does not wait timidly to jump until all the others are ready to jump; he jumps now, and anticipates that life which all desire, but which most, through inertia, prejudice, insufficient knowledge, and feeble sympathy, distrust or despair of. He knows that the world runs largely on a principle of imitation, and he launches boldly his personality into society, confident of its effect in polarizing the ideas and attitudes of the wistful. Towards himself he finds gravitating the sort of people that he would find in a regenerated social order. To him come instinctively out of his reading and his listening the ideas and events that give promise of the actual realization of his ideals. In unlooked-for spots he finds the seeds of regeneration already here. In the midst of the sternest practicalities he finds blossoming those activities and personalities which the unbelieving have told him were impossible in a human world. And he finds, moreover, that it is these activities and personalities that furnish all the real joy, the real creation, the real life of the present. The prophets and the teachers he finds are with him. In his camp he finds all those writers and leaders who sway men's minds to-day and make their life, all unconscious as they are of the revolutionary character of the message, more rich and dynamic. To live this life of his vision practically here in the present is thus the exceeding great reward of radical youth. And this life, so potent and glowing amongst the crude malignity of modern life, fortifies and stimulates him, and gives him the surety, which is sturdier than any dream or hope, of the coming time when this life will permeate and pervade all society instead of only a part.

XIII

THE COLLEGE : AN INNER VIEW

XIII

THE COLLEGE: AN INNER VIEW

THE undergraduate of to-day, if he reads the magazines, discovers that a great many people are worrying seriously about his condition. College presidents and official investigators are discussing his scholarship, his extra-curricular activities, and his moral stamina. Not content with the surface of the matter, they are going deeper and are investigating the college itself, its curriculum, the scholarship of the instructors, and its adequacy in realizing its high ideal as a preparation for life. The undergraduate finds that these observers are pretty generally inclined to exonerate him for many of his shortcomings, and to lay the blame on the college itself; the system is indicted, and not the helpless product.

For this he is grateful, and he realizes that this dissatisfaction among educators, this uneasy searching of the academic heart, promises well for the education of his children, and for himself if he remains in college long enough to get the benefit of the reforms. Meanwhile, as he attends recitations and meetings of undergraduate societies, talks with his fellow students and the professors, and reads the college papers, he may, even if he can get no hint of the mysterious inner circles where the destinies of the students are shaped and great questions of policy decided, be able himself to see some of the things that complicate college scholarship to-day, from an inner point of view which is impossible to the observer looking down from above. He may find in the character of the student body itself, and the way in which it reacts to what the college offers it, an explanation of some of the complications of scholarship that so disturb our critics; and in a certain new quality in the spirit of the college, something that is beginning to crystallize his own ideals, and to make him count himself fortunate that he is receiving his education in this age and no other. In the constitution of college society, and in the intellectual and spiritual ideals of the teachers, he may find the explanation of why the college is as it is, and the inspiration of what the college ought to be and is coming to be.

The first thing that is likely to impress the undergraduate is the observation that college society is much less democratic than it used to

314

be. It is to be expected, of course, that it will be simply an epitome of the society round about it. But the point is, that whereas the college of the past was probably more democratic than the society about it, the present-day college is very much less democratic. Democracy does not require uniformity, but it does require a certain homogeneity, and the college to-day is less homogeneous than that of our fathers. For the growing preponderance of the cities has meant that an ever-increasing proportion of city-bred men go to college, in contrast to the past, when the men were drawn chiefly from the small towns and country districts. Since social distinctions are very much more sharply marked in the city than in the country, this trend has been a potent influence in undemocratizing the college. In ordinary city life these distinctions are not yet, at least, insistent enough to cause any particular class feeling, but in the ideal world of college life they become aggravated, and sufficiently acute to cause much misunderstanding and ill-feeling. With increasing fashionableness, the small college, until recently the stronghold of democracy, is beginning to succumb, and to acquire all those delicately devised, subtle forms of snobbery which have hitherto characterized the life of the large college. If this tendency continues, the large college will have a decided advantage as a preparation for life, for as a rule it is situated in a large city, where the environment more nearly approximates the environment of after life than does the artificial and sheltered life of the small college.

The presence of aliens in large numbers in the big colleges, and increasingly in the smaller colleges, is an additional factor in complicating the social situation. It ought not to be ignored, for it has important results in making the college considerably less democratic even than would otherwise be the case. It puts the American representatives on the defensive, so that they draw still more closely together for self-defense, and pull more tightly their lines of vested interest and social and political privilege. The prejudice of race can always be successfully appealed to in undergraduate matters, even to the extent of beguiling many men with naturally democratic consciences into doing things which they would murmur at if called on to do as individuals, and not as the protectors of the social prestige of the college. The fraternities are of course the centre of this vast political system which fills the ath-

letic managerships, selects members of the societies, officers of classes and clubs, editors and as-
sistants of publications, and performs generally
all that indispensable public service of excluding
the aliens, the unpresentable, and the generally
unemployable from activity.

I am aware that most of the colleges pride themselves on the fact that the poor man has an equal
chance with the rich to-day to win extra-curricular honors, and mingle in college society on a perfect plane of social equality with the best. It is
true, of course, that in college as in real life the
exceptional man will always rise to the top. But
this does not alter the fact that there exists at too
many American colleges a wholesale disfranchise-
ment from any participation in the extra-curricular activities, that is not based on any recognizable
principle of talent or ability. It is all probably
inherent in the nature of things, and to cavil at it
sets one down as childish and unpractical. At present it certainly seems inevitable and unalterable.
The organized efforts of the President recently to
democratize the social situation at Princeton met
with such dull, persistent hostility on the part of
the alumni that they had to be abandoned.

This social situation in the college is not very

often mentioned in the usual discussions of college problems, but I have dwelt on it here at length because I believe that it has a direct bearing on scholarship. For it creates an eternal and irreconcilable conflict between scholarship and extra-curricular activities. Scholarship is fundamentally democratic. Before the bar of marks and grades, penniless adventurer and rich man's son stand equal. In college society, therefore, with its sharply marked social distinctions, scholarship fails to provide a satisfactory field for honor and reputation. This implies no dislike to scholarship as such on the part of the ruling class in college society, but means simply that scholarship forces an unwelcome democratic standard on a naturally undemocratic society. This class turns therefore to the extra-curricular activities as a superior field for distinction, a field where honor will be done a man, not only for his ability, but for the undefinable social prestige which he brings along with him to college from the outside world. There is thus a division of functions, — the socially fit take the fraternities, the managerships, the publications, the societies; the unpresentable take the honors and rewards of scholarship. Each class probably gets just what it needs for after life.

The division would thus be palpably fair were it not for the fact that an invidious distinction gets attached to the extra-curricular activities, which turns the energy of many of the most capable and talented men, men with real personality and powers of leadership, men without a taint of snobbery, into a mad scramble for these outside places, with consequent, but quite unintentional, bad effects on their scholarship.

The result of all this is, of course, a general lowering of scholarship in the college. The ruling class is content with passing marks, and has no ambition to excel in scholarship, for it does not feel that the attainment of scholars' honors confers the distinctions upon it that it desires. In addition, this listlessness for scholarship serves to retard the work of the scholarly portion of the classes; it makes the instructor work harder, and clogs up generally the work of the course. This listlessness may be partly due to another factor in the situation. An ever larger proportion of college students to-day comes from the business class, where fifty years ago it came from the professional class. This means a difference between the intellectual background of the home that the man leaves and of the college to which he comes, very much greater than when college training was still pretty much the exclusive property of the professional man or the solid merchant, and almost an hereditary matter. For, nowadays, probably a majority of undergraduates are sent to college by fathers who have not had a college education themselves, but who, reverencing, as all Americans do, Education if not Learning, are ambitious that their sons shall have its benefits. These parents can well afford to set their sons up handsomely so that they shall lose nothing of the well-rounded training that makes up college life; and although it is doubtful whether their idea of the result is much more than a vague feeling that college will give their boys tone,.and polish them off much in the way that the young ladies' boarding-school polishes off the girls, they are a serious factor to be reckoned with in any discussion of college problems.

Most of these young men come thus from homes of conventional religion, cheap literature, and lack of intellectual atmosphere, bring few intellectual acquisitions with them, and, since they are most of them going into business, and will therefore make little practical use of these acquisitions in after life, contrive to carry a minimum

away with them. In the college courses and talks
with their instructors they come into an intellectual atmosphere that is so utterly different from
what they have been accustomed to that, instead
of an intellectual sympathy between instructor
and student, there ensues an intellectual struggle
that is demoralizing to both. The instructor has
sometimes to carry on a veritable guerilla warfare
of new ideas against the pupils in his courses, with
a disintegrating effect that is often far from happy.
If he does not disintegrate, he too often stiffens
the youth, if of the usually tough traditional cast
of mind, into an impregnable resolution that de-
fies all new ideas forever after. This divergence
of ideals and attitudes toward life is one of the
most interesting complications of scholarship, for
it is dramatic and flashes out in the class-room,
in aspects at times almost startling.

There is still another thing that complicates
scholarship, at least in the larger colleges that
have professional schools. Two or three years
of regular college work are now required to enter
the schools of law, medicine, divinity, and education. An undergraduate who looks forward to
entering these professional schools, too often sees
this period of college work as a necessary but

troublesome evil which must be gone through with as speedily as possible. In his headlong rush he is apt to slight his work, or take a badly synthesized course of studies, or, in an effort to get all he can while he is in the college, to gorge himself with a mass of material that cannot possibly be digested. Now, the college work is of course only prescribed in order that the professional man may have a broad background of general culture before he begins to specialize. Any hurrying through defeats this purpose, and renders this preliminary work worse than useless. A college course must have a chance to digest if it is to be at all profitable to a man; and digestion takes time. Between the listlessness of the business youths who have no particular interest in scholarship, and the impetuosity of the prospective professional man who wants to get at his tools, the ordinary scholar who wants to learn to think, to get a robust sort of culture in an orderly and leisurely way, and feel his mental muscles growing month by month, gets the worst of it, or at least has little attention paid to him. The instructor is so busy, drumming on the laggards or restraining the reckless, that the scholar has to work out much of his own salvation alone.

Whether or not all this is good for the scholar in cultivating his self-reliance, the general level of scholarship certainly suffers. Neither the college administration nor the faculties have been entirely guiltless, in the past, of yielding before the rising tide of extra-curricular activities. Athletics, through the protection, supervision, and even financial assistance, of the college, have become a thoroughly unwholesome excrescence on college life. They have become the nucleus for a perverted college sentiment. College spirit has come to mean enthusiasm for the winning of a game, and a college that has no football team is supposed to have necessarily no college spirit. Pride and loyalty to Alma Mater, the prestige of one's college, one's own collegiate self-respect, get bound up and dependent upon a winning season at athletics. It seems amazing sometimes to the undergraduate how the college has surrendered to the student point of view. Instructors too often, in meeting students informally, assume that they must talk about what is supposed to interest the student rather than their own intellectual interests. They do not deceive the student, and they do miss a real opportunity to impress their personality upon him and to awaken him to a recognition of a broader world of vital interests than athletic scores and records.

If the college would take away its patronage of athletics, which puts a direct premium on semi-professionalism, would circumscribe the club-house features of the fraternities, and force some more democratic method of selection on the undergraduate societies, would it have the effect of raising the general level of scholarship? It surely seems that such a movement on the part of the college administration would result in keeping athletics proportioned directly to the interest that the student body took in it, to the extent of their participation in it, and the voluntary support that they gave to it, instead of to the amount of money that an army of graduate managers and alumni associations can raise for it and to the exertions of paid professional coaches and volunteer rah-rah boys. This would permit college sentiment to flow back into its natural channels, so that the undergraduate might begin to feel some pride in the cultural prestige of his college, and acquire a new respect for the scholarly achievements of its big men. This would mean an awakened interest in scholarship. The limitation of extra-curricular activities would mean that

that field would become less adequate as a place for acquiring distinction; opportunity would be diminished, and it would become more and more difficult to maintain social eminence as the *sine qua non* of campus distinction. Who knows but what these activities might be finally abandoned entirely to the unpresentable class, and the ruling class seize upon the field of scholarship as a surer way of acquiring distinction, since the old gods had fled?

If the college is not yet ready to adopt so drastic an attitude, it has at least already begun to preach democracy. It is willing to preach inspirationally what it cannot yet do actively. In the last few years there has been creeping into the colleges in the person of the younger teachers a new spirit of positive conviction, a new enthusiasm, that makes a college education to-day a real inspiration to the man who can catch the message. And at the risk of being considered a traitor to his class, the sincere undergraduate of to-day must realize the changed attitude, and ally himself with his radical teachers in spirit and activity. He then gets an altered view of college life. He begins to see the college course as an attempt, as yet not fully organized but becoming surer of its purpose as time goes on, to convert the heterogeneous mass of American youth — scions of a property-getting class with an antiquated tradition and ideals that are out of harmony with the ideals of the leaders of thought to-day; slightly dispirited aliens, whose racial ideals have been torn and confused by the disintegrating influences of American life; men of hereditary culture; penniless adventurers hewing upward to a profession — to a democratic, realistic, scientific attitude toward life that will harmonize and explain the world as a man looks at it, enable him to interpret human nature in terms of history and the potentialities of the future, and furnish as solid and sure an intellectual and spiritual support as the old religious background of our fathers that has been fading these many years.

This is the work of the college of to-day, as it was the work of the college of fifty years ago to justify the works of God to man. The college thus becomes for the first time in American history a reorganizing force. It has become thoroughly secularized these last twenty years, and now finds arrayed against it, in spirit at least if not in open antagonism, the churches and the conservative moulders of opinion. The college has a great opportunity before it to become, not only the teacher, but the inspirational centre of the thought and ideals of the time.

If to the rising generation our elders rarely seem quite contemporaneous in their criticisms of things, we in turn are apt to take the ordinary for the unique. We may be simply reading into the college our own enthusiasms, and may attribute to the college a new attitude when it is ourselves that are different. But I am sure that some such ideal is vaguely beginning to crystallize in the minds of the younger professors and the older undergraduates, or those who have been out in the world long enough to get a slightly objective point of view. The passing of the classics has meant much more than a mere change in the curriculum of the college; it has meant a complete shifting of attitude. The classics as a cultural core about which the other disciplines were built up have given place to the social sciences, especially history, which is hailed now by some of its enthusiastic devotees as the sum of all knowledge. The union of humanistic spirit with scientific point of view, which has been longed for these many years, seems on the point of being actually achieved, and it is the new spirit that the colleges seem to be propagating.

I am sure that it is a democratic spirit. History, economics, and the other social sciences are presented as the record of the development of human freedom, and the science of man's social life. We are told to look on institutions not as rigid and eternally fixed, but as fluid and in the course of evolution to an ever higher cultivation of individuality and general happiness, and to cast our thinking on public questions into this new mould. A college man is certainly not educated to-day unless he gets this democratic attitude. That is what makes the aristocratic organization of undergraduate life doubly unfortunate. For one of the most valuable opportunities of college life is the chance to get acquainted, not politely and distantly, but intimately, with all types of men and minds from all parts of the country and all classes of society, so that one may learn what the young men of the generation are really thinking and hoping. Knowledge of men is an indispensable feature of a real education: not a knowledge of their weaknesses, as too many seem to mean by the phrase, but knowledge of their strength and capabilities, so that one may get the broadest possible sympathy with human life as it is actually lived to-day, and not as it is seen through the idealistic glasses of former generations. The association only with men of one's own class, such as the organization of college life to-day fosters, is simply fatal to any broad understanding of life. The refusal to make the acquaintance while in college of as many as possible original, self-dependent personalities, regardless of race and social status, is morally suicidal. There are indications, however, that the preaching of the democratic gospel is beginning to have its influence, in the springing-up of college forums and societies which do without the rigid coöptation that has cultivated the cutting one's self off from one's fellows.

I am sure that it is a scientific spirit. The scientific attitude toward life is no longer kept as the exclusive property of the technical schools. It has found its way into those studies that have been known as humanistic, but, in penetrating, it has become colored itself, so that the student is shown the world, not as a relentless machine, running according to mechanical laws, but as an organism, profoundly modifiable and directive by human will and purpose. He learns that the world in which he lives is truly a mechanism, but a mechanism that exists for the purpose of turning out products as man shall direct for the enrichment of his own life. He learns to appreciate more the application to social life of machinery in organization and coöperation; he gets some idea of the forces that build up human nature and sway men's actions. He acquires an impartial way of looking at things; effort is made to get him to separate his personal prejudices from the larger view, and get an objective vision of men and events. The college endeavors with might and main to cultivate in him an open-mindedness, so that at twenty-five he will not close up to the entrance of new ideas, but will find his college course merely introductory to life, a learning of one's bearings in a great world of thought and activity, and an inspiration to a constant working for better things.

I am sure that it is a critical spirit. A critical attitude toward life is as bad a thing for a boy as it is an indispensable thing for an educated man. The college tries to cultivate it gradually in its students, so that by the end of his four years a man will have come simply not to take everything for granted, but to test and weigh and prove ideas and institutions with which he comes in contact. Of course the results are unfortunate when this critical attitude comes with a sudden shock so as to be a mere disillusionment, the turning yellow of a beautiful world; but it must come if a man is to see wisely and understand. The college must teach him to criticize without rancor, and see that his cynicism, if that must come too, is purging and cleansing and not bitter.

And lastly, I am sure that it is an enthusiastic spirit. The college wants to give a man a keen desire for social progress, a love for the arts, a delight in sheer thinking, and a confidence in his own powers. It will do little good to teach a man about what men have thought and done and built unless some spark is kindled, some reaction produced that will have consequences for the future; it will do little good to teach him about literature and the arts unless some kind of an emotional push is imparted to him that will drive him on to teach himself further and grow into a larger appreciation of the best; it will do little good to enforce scientific discipline unless by it the mind is forged into a keener weapon for attacking problems and solving them scientifically and not superficially. And it is just this enthusiasm that the college, and only the college, can impart. We come there to learn from men, not from books.

331

We could learn from books as well at home, but years of individual study will not equal the inspirational value of one short term of listening to the words of a wise and good man. Only enthusiasm can knit the scattered ideals and timorous aspirations into a constructive whole.

Some such spirit as I have endeavored to outline, the college is beginning to be infused with to-day; some such spirit the undergraduate must get if he is to be in the best sense educated and adequately equipped for the complex work of the world. If such a spirit is instilled, it almost matters little what the details of his courses are, or the mere material of his knowledge. Such an attitude will be a sufficient preparation for life, and adequate training for citizenship. We want citizens who are enthusiastic thinkers, not docile and uncritical followers of tradition; we want leaders of public opinion with the scientific point of view: unclassed men, not men like the leaders of the passing generation, saturated with class prejudices and class ideals.

The college is rapidly revising its curriculum in line with the new standards. The movement is so new, to be sure, that things have hardly got their bearings yet. Men who graduated only ten years ago tell me that there was nothing like this new spirit when they were in college. The student finds a glut of courses, and flounders around for two or three years before he gets any poise at all. A judicious mixture of compulsory and elective courses seems to be furnishing a helpful guide, and a system of honor courses like that recently introduced at Columbia provides an admirable means, not only to a more intensive culture, but also to the synthesis of intellectual interests that creates a definite attitude toward life, and yet for the absence of which so many young men of ability and power stand helpless and undecided on the threshold of active life. To replace the classics, now irretrievably gone as the backbone of the curriculum, the study of history seems an admirable discipline, besides furnishing the indispensable background for the literary and philosophical studies. Scientific ethics and social psychology should occupy an important place in the revised curriculum. The college cannot afford to leave the undergraduate to the mercies of conventional religion and a shifting moral tradition.

The pedantic, Germanistic type of scholarship is rapidly passing. The divisions between the departments are beginning to break down. Already the younger instructors are finding their ideal professor in the man who, while he knows one branch thoroughly, is interested in a wide range of subjects. The departments are reacting upon one another; both undergraduates and instructors are coming to see intellectual life as a whole, and not as a miscellaneous collection of specialized chunks of knowledge. The type of man is becoming common who could go to almost any other department of the college and give a suggestive and interesting, if not erudite, lecture on some subject in connection with its work. It is becoming more and more common now that when you touch a professor you touch a man and not an intellectual specialty.

The undergraduate himself is beginning to react strongly to this sort of scholarship. He catches an inspiration from the men in the faculty who exhibit it, and he is becoming expert in separating the sheep from the goats. He does not want experiments in educational psychology tried upon him: all he demands in his teacher is personality. He wants to feel that the instructor is not simply passing on dead knowledge in the form it was passed on to him, but that he has assimilated it and has read his own experience into it, so that

334

it has come to mean more to him than almost anything in the world.

Professors are fond of saying that they like to have their students react to what they bring them; the student in turn likes to feel that the professor himself has reacted to what he is teaching. Otherwise his teaching is very apt to be in vain. American youth are very much less docile than they used to be, and they are little content any longer to have second-hand knowledge, a little damaged in transit, thrust upon them. The undergraduate wants to feel that the instructor is giving him his best all the time, a piece out of the very warp and woof of his own thinking.

The problem of the college in the immediate future is thus to make these ideals good, to permeate undergraduate society with the new spirit, and to raise the level of scholarship by making learning not an end in itself but a means to life. The curriculum and administrative routine will be seen simply as means to the cultivation of an attitude towards life. As the ideals crystallize out and the college becomes surer and surer of its purpose, it will find itself leading the thought of the age in new channels of conviction and constructive statesmanship through its inspirational influence on the young men of the time. Admitting that these ideals are still unorganized and unestablished, that in many of the colleges they have hardly begun to appear, while even in the larger ones they are little more than tendencies as yet, — is it too much to hope that a few years will see the college conscious of its purpose, and already beginning to impose on the rank and file of its members, instructors and undergraduates alike, the ideals which have been felt this last decade by the more sensitive?

XIV

A PHILOSOPHY OF HANDICAP

XIV

A PHILOSOPHY OF HANDICAP

IT would not perhaps be thought, ordinarily,
that the man whom physical disabilities have
made so helpless that he is unable to move around
among his fellows, can bear his lot more happily,
even though he suffer pain, and face life with a
more cheerful and contented spirit, than can
the man whose handicaps are merely enough to
mark him out from the rest of his fellows without
preventing him from entering with them into
most of their common affairs and experiences. But
the fact is that the former's very helplessness
makes him content to rest and not to strive. I
know a young man so helplessly disabled that he
has to be carried about, who is happy in reading
a little, playing chess, taking a course or two in
college, and all with the sunniest good-will in the
world, and a happiness that seems strange and
unaccountable to my restlessness. He does not
cry for the moon.

When the handicapped youth, however, is in full
possession of his faculties, and can move about

freely, he is perforce drawn into all the currents of life. Particularly if he has his own way in the world to make, his road is apt to be hard and rugged, and he will penetrate to an unusual depth in his interpretation both of the world's attitude toward such misfortunes, and of the attitude toward the world which such misfortunes tend to cultivate in men like him. For he has all the battles of a stronger man to fight, and he is at a double disadvantage in fighting them. He has constantly with him the sense of being obliged to make extra efforts to overcome the bad impression of his physical defects, and he is haunted with a constant feeling of weakness and low vitality which makes effort more difficult and renders him easily fainthearted and discouraged by failure. He is never confident of himself, because he has grown up in an atmosphere where nobody has been very confident of him; and yet his environment and circumstances call out all sorts of ambitions and energies in him which, from the nature of his case, are bound to be immediately thwarted. This attitude is likely to keep him at a generally low level of accomplishment unless he have an unusually strong will, and a strong will is perhaps the last thing to develop under such circumstances.

A PHILOSOPHY OF HANDICAP

The handicapped man is always conscious that the world does not expect very much from him. And it takes him a long time to see in this a challenge instead of a firm pressing down to a low level of accomplishment. As a result, he does not expect very much of himself; he is timid in approaching people, and distrustful of his ability to persuade and convince. He becomes extraordinarily sensitive to other people's first impressions of him. Those who are to be his friends he knows instantly, and further acquaintance adds little to the intimacy and warm friendship that he at once feels for them. On the other hand, those who do not respond to him immediately cannot by any effort either on his part or theirs overcome that first alienation.

This sensitiveness has both its good and its bad sides. It makes friendship the most precious thing in the world to him, and he finds that he arrives at a much richer and wider intimacy with his friends than do ordinary men with their light, surface friendships, based on good fellowship or the convenience of the moment. But on the other hand this sensitiveness absolutely unfits him for business and the practice of a profession, where one must be "all things to all men," and the professional manner is indispensable to success. For here, where he has to meet a constant stream of men of all sorts and conditions, his sensitiveness to these first impressions will make his case hopeless. Except with those few who by some secret sympathy will seem to respond, his physical deficiencies will stand like a huge barrier between his personality and other men's. The magical good fortune of attractive personal appearance makes its way almost without effort in the world, breaking down all sorts of walls of disapproval and lack of interest. Even the homely person can attract by personal charm.

The doors of the handicapped man are always locked, and the key is on the outside. He may have treasures of charm inside, but they will never be revealed unless the person outside coöperates with him in unlocking the door. A friend becomes, to a much greater degree than with the ordinary man, the indispensable means of discovering one's own personality. One only exists, so to speak, with friends. It is easy to see how hopelessly such a sensitiveness incapacitates a man for business, professional or social life, where the hasty and superficial impression is everything, and disaster is the fate of the man who has not all the treasures of his personality in the front window, where they can be readily inspected and appraised.

It thus takes the handicapped man a long time to get adjusted to his world. Childhood is perhaps the hardest time of all. As a child he is a strange creature in a strange land. It was my own fate to be just strong enough to play about with the other boys, and attempt all their games and "stunts," without being strong enough actually to succeed in any of them. It never used to occur to me that my failures and lack of skill were due to circumstances beyond my control, but I would always impute them, in consequence of my rigid Calvinistic bringing-up, I suppose, to some moral weakness of my own. I suffered tortures in trying to learn to skate, to climb trees, to play ball, to conform in general to the ways of the world. I never resigned myself to the inevitable, but over-exerted myself constantly in a grim determination to succeed. I was good at my lessons, and through timidity rather than priggishness, I hope, a very well-behaved boy at school; I was devoted, too, to music, and learned to play the piano pretty well. But I despised my reputation for excellence in these things, and instead of adapting myself philosophically to the situation, I strove and have been striving ever since to do the things I could not.

As I look back now it seems perfectly natural that I should have followed the standards of the crowd, and loathed my high marks in lessons and deportment, and the concerts to which I was sent by my aunt, and the exhibitions of my musical skill that I had to give before admiring ladies. Whether or not such an experience is typical of handicapped children, there is tragedy there for those situated as I was. For had I been a little weaker physically, I should have been thrown back on reading omnivorously and cultivating my music, with some possible results; while if I had been a little stronger, I could have participated in the play on an equal footing with the rest. As it was, I simply tantalized myself, and grew up with a deepening sense of failure, and a lack of pride in that at which I really excelled.

When the world became one of dances and parties and social evenings and boy-and-girl attachments, — the world of youth, — I was to find myself still less adapted to it. And this was the harder to bear because I was naturally sociable, and all these things appealed tremendously to me. This world of admiration and gayety and smiles and favors and quick interest and companionship, however, is only for the well-begotten and the debonair. It was not through any cruelty or dislike, I think, that I was refused admittance; indeed they were always very kind about inviting me. But it was more as if a ragged urchin had been asked to come and look through the window at the light and warmth of a glittering party; I was truly in the world, but not of the world. Indeed there were times when one would almost prefer conscious cruelty to this silent, unconscious, gentle oblivion. And this is the tragedy, I suppose, of all the ill-favored and unattractive to a greater or less degree; the world of youth is a world of so many conventions, and the abnormal in any direction is so glaringly and hideously abnormal.

Although it took me a long time to understand this, and I continued to attribute my failure mostly to my own character, trying hard to compensate for my physical deficiencies by skill and cleverness, I suffered comparatively few pangs, and got much better adjusted to this world than to the other. For I was older, and I had acquired a lively interest in all the social politics; I would get so interested in watching how people behaved, and in sizing them up, that only at rare intervals

would I remember that I was really having no
hand in the game. This interest just in the ways
people are human, has become more and more a
positive advantage in my life, and has kept sweet
many a situation that might easily have cost me a
pang. Not that a person with disabilities should
be a sort of detective, evil-mindedly using his social opportunities for spying out and analyzing his
friends' foibles, but that, if he does acquire an interest in people quite apart from their relation
to him, he may go into society with an easy
conscience and a certainty that he will be enter-
tained and possibly entertaining, even though he
cuts a poor enough social figure. He must simply
not expect too much.

Perhaps the bitterest struggles of the handicapped man come when he tackles the business
world. If he has to go out for himself to look for
work, without fortune, training, or influence, as
I personally did, his way will indeed be rugged.
His disability will work against him for any position where he must be much in the eyes of men,
and his general insignificance has a subtle influence in convincing those to whom he applies that
he is unfitted for any kind of work. As I have
suggested, his keen sensitiveness to other people's

impressions of him makes him more than usually timid and unable to counteract that fatal first impression by any display of personal force and will. He cannot get his personality over across that barrier. The cards seem stacked against him from the start. With training and influence something might be done, but alone and unaided his case is almost hopeless. The attitude toward him ranges from, "You can't expect us to create a place for you," to, "How could it enter your head that we should find any use for you?" He is discounted at the start: it is not business to make allowances for anybody; and while people are not cruel or unkind, it is the hopeless finality of the thing that fills one's heart with despair.

The environment of a big city is perhaps the worst possible that a man in such a situation could have. For the thousands of seeming opportunities lead one restlessly on and on, and keep one's mind perpetually unsettled and depressed. There is a poignant mental torture that comes with such an experience, — the urgent need, the repeated failure, or rather the repeated failure even to obtain a chance to fail, the realization that those at home can ill afford to have you idle, the growing dread of encountering people, — all this is something that those who have never been through it can never realize. Personally I know of no particular way of escape. One can expect to do little by one's own unaided efforts. I solved my difficulties only by evading them, by throwing overboard some of my responsibility, and taking the desperate step of entering college on a scholarship. Desultory work is not nearly so humiliating when one is using one's time to some advantage, and college furnishes an ideal environment where the things at which a man handicapped like myself can succeed really count. One's self-respect can begin to grow like a weed.

For at the bottom of all the difficulties of a man like me is really the fact that his self-respect is so slow in growing up. Accustomed from childhood to being discounted, his self-respect is not naturally very strong, and it would require pretty constant success in a congenial line of work really to confirm it. If he could only more easily separate the factors that are due to his physical disability from those that are due to his weak will and character, he might more quickly attain self-respect, for he would realize what he is responsible for, and what he is not. But at the beginning he rarely makes allowances for himself; he is his own severest judge. He longs for a "strong will," and yet the experience of having his efforts promptly nipped off at the beginning is the last thing on earth to produce that will.

If the handicapped youth is brought into harsh and direct touch with the real world, life proves a much more complex thing to him than to the ordinary man. Many of his inherited platitudes vanish at the first touch. Life appears to him as a grim struggle, where ability does not necessarily mean opportunity and success, nor piety sympathy, and where helplessness cannot count on assistance and kindly interest. Human affairs seem to be running on a wholly irrational plan, and success to be founded on chance as much as on anything. But if he can stand the first shock of disillusionment, he may find himself enormously interested in discovering how they actually do run, and he will want to burrow into the motives of men, and find the reasons for the crass inequalities and injustices of the world he sees around him. He has practically to construct anew a world of his own, and explain a great many things to himself that the ordinary person never dreams of finding unintelligible at all. He will be filled with a profound sympathy for all who are despised and ignored in the world. When he has been through the neglect and struggles of a handicapped and ill-favored man himself, he will begin to understand the feelings of all the horde of the unpresentable and the unemployable, the incompetent and the ugly, the queer and crotchety people who make up so large a proportion of human folk.

We are perhaps too prone to get our ideas and standards of worth from the successful, without reflecting that the interpretations of life which patriotic legend, copy-book philosophy, and the sayings of the wealthy give us, are pitifully inadequate for those who fall behind in the race. Surely there are enough people to whom the task of making a decent living and maintaining themselves and their families in their social class, or of winning and keeping the respect of their fellows, is a hard and bitter task, to make a philosophy gained through personal disability and failure as just and true a method of appraising the life around us as the cheap optimism of the ordinary professional man. And certainly a kindlier, for it has no shade of contempt or disparagement about it.

It irritates me as if I had been spoken of contemptuously myself, to hear people called "common" or "ordinary," or to see that deadly and delicate feeling for social gradations crop out, which so many of our upper middle-class women seem to have. It makes me wince to hear a man spoken of as a failure, or to have it said of one that he "does n't amount to much." Instantly I want to know why he has not succeeded, and what have been the forces that have been working against him. He is the truly interesting person, and yet how little our eager-pressing, on-rushing world cares about such aspects of life, and how hideously though unconsciously cruel and heartless it usually is!

Often I had tried in argument to show my friends how much of circumstance and chance go to the making of success; and when I reached the age of sober reading, a long series of the works of radical social philosophers, beginning with Henry George, provided me with the materials for a philosophy which explained why men were miserable and overworked, and why there was on the whole so little joy and gladness among us, — and which fixed the blame. Here was suggested a goal, and a definite glorious future, toward which all good men might work. My own working hours became filled with visions of how men could be brought to see all that this meant, and how I in particular might work some great and wonderful thing for human betterment. In more recent years, the study of history and social psychology and ethics has made those crude outlines sounder and more normal, and brought them into a saner relation to other aspects of life and thought, but I have not lost the first glow of enthusiasm, nor my belief in social progress as the first right and permanent interest for every thinking and true-hearted man or woman.

I am ashamed that my experience has given me so little chance to count in any way either toward the spreading of such a philosophy or toward direct influence and action. Nor do I yet see clearly how I shall be able to count effectually toward this ideal. Of one thing I am sure, however: that life will have little meaning for me except as I am able to contribute toward some such ideal of social betterment, if not in deed, then in word. For this is the faith that I believe we need to-day, all of us, — a truly religious belief in human progress, a thorough social consciousness, an eager delight in every sign and promise of social improvement, and best of all, a new spirit of courage that will dare. I want to give to the young men whom I see, — who, with fine intellect and high principles, lack just that light of the future on their faces that would give them a purpose and meaning in life, — to them I want to give some touch of this philosophy, that will energize their lives, and save them from the disheartening effects of that poisonous counsel of timidity and distrust of human ideals which pours out in steady stream from reactionary press and pulpit.

It is hard to tell just how much of this philosophy has been due to handicap. If it is solely to that that I owe its existence, the price has not been a heavy one to pay. For it has given me something that I should not know how to be without. For, however gained, this radical philosophy has not only made the world intelligible and dynamic to me, but has furnished me with the strongest spiritual support. I know that many people, handicapped by physical weakness and failure, find consolation and satisfaction in a very different sort of faith, — in an evangelical religion, and a feeling of close dependence on God and close communion with him. But my experience has made my ideal of character militant rather than long-suffering.

I very early experienced a revulsion against the rigid Presbyterianism in which I had been brought up, — a purely intellectual revulsion, I believe, because my mind was occupied for a long time afterwards with theological questions, and the only feeling that entered into it was a sort of disgust at the arrogance of damning so great a proportion of the human race. I read T. W. Higginson's "The Sympathy of Religions" with the greatest satisfaction, and attended the Unitarian church whenever I could slip away. This faith, while it still appeals to me, seems at times a little too static and refined to satisfy me with completeness. For some time there was a considerable bitterness in my heart at the narrowness of the people who could still find comfort in the old faith. Reading Buckle and Oliver Wendell Holmes gave me a new contempt for "conventionality," and my social philosophy still further tortured me by throwing the burden for the misery of the world on these same good neighbors. And all this, although I think I did not make a nuisance of myself, made me feel a spiritual and intellectual isolation in addition to my more or less effective physical isolation.

Happily these days are over. The world has righted itself, and I have been able to appreciate and realize how people count in a social and

354

group capacity as well as in an individual and personal one, and to separate the two in my thinking.
Really to believe in human nature while striving
to know the thousand forces that warp it from its
ideal development, — to call for and expect much
from men and women, and not to be disappointed
and embittered if they fall short, — to try to do
good with people rather than to them, — this is
my religion on its human side. And if God exists,
I think that He must be in the warm sun, in the
kindly actions of the people we know and read
of, in the beautiful things of art and nature, and
in the closeness of friendships. He may also be in
heaven, in life, in suffering, but it is only in these
simple moments of happiness that I feel Him and
know that He is there.

Death I do not understand at all. I have seen
it in its cruelest, most irrational forms, where
there has seemed no excuse, no palliation. I have
only known that if we were more careful, and
more relentless in fighting evil, if we knew more
of medical science, such things would not be. I
know that a sound body, intelligent care and
training, prolong life, and that the death of a very
old person is neither sad nor shocking, but sweet
and fitting. I see in death a perpetual warning of

how much there is to be known and done in the way of human progress and betterment. And equally, it seems to me, is this true of disease. So all the crises and deeper implications of life seem inevitably to lead back to that question of social improvement, and militant learning and doing.

This, then, is the goal of my religion, — the bringing of fuller, richer life to more people on this earth. All institutions and all works that do not have this for their object are useless and pernicious. And this is not to be a mere philosophic precept which may well be buried under a host of more immediate matter, but a living faith, to permeate one's thought, and transfuse one's life. Prevention must be the method against evil. To remove temptation from men, and to apply the stimulus which shall call forth their highest endeavors, — these seem to me the only right principles of ethical endeavor. Not to keep waging the age-long battle with sin and poverty, but to make the air around men so pure that foul lungs cannot breathe it, — this should be our noblest religious aim.

Education, knowledge and training, — I have felt so keenly my lack of these things that I count them as the greatest of means toward making life

noble and happy. The lack of stimulus has tended
with me to dissipate the power which might otherwise have been concentrated in some one productive direction. Or perhaps it was the many weak
stimuli that constantly incited me and thus kept
me from following one particular bent. I look
back on what seems a long waste of intellectual
power, time frittered away in groping and mop-
ing, which might easily have been spent con-
structively. A defect in one of the physical senses
often means a keener sensitiveness in the others,
but it seems that unless the sphere of action that
the handicapped man has is very much narrowed,
his intellectual ability will not grow in compensation for his physical defects. He will always feel
that, had he been strong or even successful, he
would have been further advanced intellectually,
and would have attained greater command over
his powers. For his mind tends to be cultivated
extensively, rather than intensively. He has so
many problems to meet, so many things to explain to himself, that he acquires a wide rather
than a profound knowledge. Perhaps eventually,
by eliminating most of these interests as practicable fields, he may tie himself down to one line
of work; but at first he is pretty apt to find his

mind rebellious. If he is eager and active, he will get a smattering of too many things, and his imperfect, badly trained organism will make intense application very difficult.

Now that I have talked a little of my philosophy of life, particularly about what I want to put into it, there is something to be said also of its enjoyment, and what I may hope to get out of it. I have said that my ideal of character was militant rather than long-suffering. It is true that my world has been one of failure and deficit, — I have accomplished practically nothing alone, and until my college life freed me could count only two or three instances where I had received kindly counsel and suggestion; moreover it still seems a miracle to me that money can be spent for anything beyond the necessities without being first carefully weighed and pondered over, — but it has not been a world of suffering and sacrifice, my health has been almost criminally perfect in the light of my actual achievement, and life has appeared to me, at least since my more pressing responsibilities were removed, as a challenge and an arena, rather than a vale of tears. I do not like the idea of helplessly suffering one's misfortunes, of passively bearing one's lot. The Stoics

358

depress me. I do not want to look on my life as an eternal making the best of a bad bargain. Granting all the circumstances, admitting all my disabilities, I want too to "warm both hands before the fire of life." What satisfactions I have, and they are many and precious, I do not want to look on as compensations, but as positive goods.

The difference between what the strongest of the strong and the most winning of the attractive can get out of life, and what I can, is after all so slight. Our experiences and enjoyments, both his and mine, are so infinitesimal compared with the great mass of possibilities; and there must be a division of labor. If he takes the world of physical satisfactions and of material success, I at least can occupy the far richer kingdom of mental effort and artistic appreciation. And on the side of what we are to put·into life, although I admit that achievement on my part will be harder relatively to encompass than on his, at least I may have the field of artistic creation and intellectual achievement for my own. Indeed, as one gets older, the fact of one's disabilities fades dimmer and dimmer away from consciousness. One's enemy is now one's own weak will, and the struggle is to attain the artistic ideal one has set.

But one must have grown up, to get this attitude. And that is the best thing the handicapped man can do. Growing up will have given him one of the greatest satisfactions of his life, and certainly the most durable one. It will mean at least that he is out of the woods. Childhood has nothing to offer him; youth little more. They are things to be gotten through with as soon as possible. For he will not understand, and he will not be understood. He finds himself simply a bundle of chaotic impulses and emotions and ambitions, very few of which, from the nature of the case, can possibly be realized or satisfied. He is bound to be at cross-grains with the world, and he has to look sharp that he does not grow up with a bad temper and a hateful disposition, and become cynical and bitter against those who turn him away. But grown up, his horizon will broaden; he will get a better perspective, and will not take the world so seriously as he used to, nor will failure frighten him so much. He can look back and see how inevitable it all was, and understand how precarious and problematic even the best regulated of human affairs may be. And if he feels that there were

times when he should have been able to count
upon the help and kindly counsel of relatives and
acquaintances who remained dumb and uninterested, he will not put their behavior down as proof
of the depravity of human nature, but as due
to an unfortunate blindness which it will be his
work to avoid in himself by looking out for others
when he has the power.

When he has grown up, he will find that people
of his own age and experience are willing to make
those large allowances for what is out of the ordinary, which were impossible to his younger
friends, and that grown-up people touch each
other on planes other than the purely superficial.
With a broadening of his own interests, he will
find himself overlapping other people's personalities at new points, and will discover with rare
delight that he is beginning to be understood and
appreciated, — at least to a greater degree than
when he had to keep his real interests hid as something unusual. For he will begin to see in his
friends, his music and books, and his interest in
people and social betterment, his true life; many
of his restless ambitions will fade gradually away,
and he will come to recognize all the more clearly
some true ambition of his life that is within the

range of his capabilities. He will have built up his world, and have sifted out the things that are not going to concern him, and participation in which will only serve to vex and harass him. He may well come to count his disabilities even as a blessing, for it has made impossible to him at last many things in the pursuit of which he would only fritter away his time and dissipate his interest. He must not think of "resigning himself to his fate"; above all, he must insist on his own personality. For once really grown up, he will find that he has acquired self-respect and personality. Grown-upness, I think, is not a mere question of age, but of being able to look back and understand and find satisfaction in one's experience, no matter how bitter it may have been.

So to all the handicapped and the unappreciated, I would say, — Grow up as fast as you can. Cultivate the widest interests you can, and cherish all your friends. Cultivate some artistic talent, for you will find it the most durable of satisfactions, and perhaps one of the surest means of livelihood as well. Achievement is, of course, on the knees of the gods; but you will at least have the thrill of trial, and, after all, not to try is to fail. Taking your disabilities for granted, and assuming con-

stantly that they are being taken for granted, make
your social intercourse as broad and as constant
as possible. Do not take the world too seriously,
nor let too many social conventions oppress you.
Keep sweet your sense of humor, and above all
do not let any morbid feelings of inferiority creep
into your soul. You will find yourself sensitive
enough to the sympathy of others, and if you do
not find people who like you and are willing to
meet you more than halfway, it will be because
you have let your disability narrow your vision
and shrink up your soul. It will be really your
own fault, and not that of your circumstances. In
a word, keep looking outward; look out eagerly
for those things that interest you, for people who
will interest ycu and be friends with you, for new
interests and for opportunities to express yourself. You will find that your disability will come
to have little meaning for you, that it will begin
to fade quite completely out of your sight; you
will wake up some fine morning and find yourself,
after all the struggles that seemed so bitter to
you, really and truly adjusted to the world.

I am perhaps not yet sufficiently out of the
wilderness to utter all these brave words. For, I
must confess, I find myself hopelessly dependent

on my friends and my environment. My friends have come to mean more to me than almost anything else in the world. If it is far harder work to make friendships quickly, at least friendships once made have a depth and intimacy quite beyond ordinary attachments. For a man such as I am has little prestige; people do not feel the need of impressing him. They are genuine and sincere, talk to him freely about themselves, and are generally far less reticent about revealing their real personality and history and aspirations. And particularly is this so in friendships with young women. I have found their friendships the most delightful and satisfying of all. For all that social convention that insists that every friendship between a young man and woman must be on a romantic basis is necessarily absent in our case. There is no fringe around us to make our acquaintance anything but a charming companionship. With all my friends, the same thing is true. The first barrier of strangeness broken down, our interest is really in each other, and not in what each is going to think of the other, how he is to be impressed, or whether we are going to fall in love with each other. When one of my friends moves away, I feel as if a

364

great hole had been left in my life. There is a whole side of my personality that I cannot express without him. I shudder to think of any change that will deprive me of their constant companionship. Without friends I feel as if even my music and books and interests would turn stale on my hands. I confess that I am not grown up enough to get along without them.

But if I am not yet out of the wilderness, at least I think I see the way to happiness. With health and a modicum of achievement, I shall not see my lot as unenviable. And if misfortune comes, it will only be something flowing from the common lot of men, not from my own particular disability. Most of the difficulties that flow from that I flatter myself I have met by this time of my twenty-fifth year, have looked full in the face, have grappled with, and find in no wise so formidable as the world usually deems them, — no bar to my real ambitions and ideals.

THE END